TO A BETTER PRACTICE

Coming Home

TO A BETTER PRACTICE

A nurturing, no-nonsense guide
to becoming a leader
and building your work family

Angela Davis Sullivan

ISBN: 978-0-9997863-7-6 (Paperback)

Library of Congress Control Number: 00000000000

Book design by WellPut Custom Content.

First printing edition 2019.

Soapbox Publishing

11959 Sunrise Plateau Dr.
Anacortes, WA 98221
soapboxpublishing.com
adaptive-dental-solutions.com

Contents

Foreword   vii

Acknowledgements   ix

Chapter 1   Showing Up for Your Home Inspection   1

Chapter 2   The Compass Circle of Accountability   15

Chapter 3   Building Your Blueprint   29

Chapter 4   Building Your Builders   43

Chapter 5   Your Hammer and Nails   59

Chapter 6   Systems: Your Load-Bearing Support   79

Chapter 7   Using the Tools You've Got   93

Chapter 8   Coming Home to Your Better Practice   113

Further Reading   121

Foreword

There's a difference between those who tell you what to do and those who help you become the person you want to be.

Angela is the second; she's the definition of a coach.

My favorite quote of hers is "If you can't play at our level, you can't play on our team."

In *Coming Home,* Angela not only gives practical tips for running a more stress-free office, but also challenges readers over and over to look in the mirror.

It's easy to point fingers, but what about *your* mindset is holding you back? Angela knows how to dig deep and influence change.

She takes fear by the horns and coaches readers how to do the Big Scary Things like fire long-time employees or handle embezzlement with professionalism and poise. Her tough love approach will push you to be better while allowing room for necessary (if not essential) slip-ups.

I've known Angela for fifteen years and I've watched her get businesses back on track, but more importantly, I've witnessed her reignite the passion of the doctors and teams she coaches, like no one I've ever seen before.

This book is loaded with ideas, practical strategies, and questions that you won't find anywhere else. For all those doctors and team members out there, who feel lost and alone—this book is a welcome mat, inviting you to come home to a better practice.

Angela is a special talent and understands from top to bottom how to influence any office into creating a dream practice!

Dr. Bruce B. Baird

Acknowledgements

To my mentors: Dr. Bruce Baird, Vicki McManus, and Patti Sooy. Thank you for encouraging me through the years.

To my friends: Kari Miller, Robyn Ramirez, Susan Leckowicz, Jackie Adame, Chris Moriarity, Jenn Janicki, Sommer Carrol, Christine Uhen, and more. Thank you for supporting me and keeping it fun!

To my parents and family--thank you for caring about my career and being interested in how I help dentists and their teams.

And, finally, to my husband, William, and my children, Hunter and Audrey: thank you for always supporting me in whatever I take on next. I can do it all because I can come home to you.

Chapter 1

Showing Up for Your Home Inspection

I waited in the car, breathing deeply to calm myself. My family had just outgrown our old home, and it was time for us to find a new one that would serve us better. We had worked hard to find one we liked, and we were invested.

Now I waited for the home inspector to arrive, so that they could go over the details of our prospective new home. I was nervous, worried about the potential flaws they might find, even though I knew that every house has flaws and that it's far better to know about them. I knew that even if it bothered me in the short term, my family's comfort and happiness in this new home depended on a rigorous inspection to identify repairs. Ignoring the problems in the house would only lead to suffering down the road.

I always tell my clients that running a practice is a lot like taking care of a family. When things are going well, it can be just as rewarding; when things are a struggle, everything's a struggle.

I was eager to get my family into a new home that would bless us and help us to do more of the things we needed to do in our full, busy lives. Having our new home inspected was a major step in this process, and key to that step was this: showing up.

When I say *showing up*, what I mean is being willing to be part of making your practice a better place, by providing both your literal and emotional presence. It's the opposite of avoidance and fear. That willingness is expressed in an openness to admitting when things aren't great, and a desire to make things better. Willingness means you are open to accountability and change.

Brené Brown says, "The willingness to show up changes us. It makes us a little braver each time."

Just by reading this, you are already accomplishing the first step in your process to repair your practice. *You are showing up.* Well done, you.

What keeps someone from showing up?

What Keeps Us from Showing Up: The F-Word

I tried to break it to Dr. Brown gently: "Dr. Brown, your receptionist is stealing from you."

"I know," Doctor Brown said.

"What?" I asked, taken aback. "You knew?"

"There's nothing I can do about it," she said, looking away. "So there isn't any point in noticing it anymore."

"Dr. Brown," I said, "I'm concerned about you. You can't work with someone you can't trust. Look, I can help you. I can help you practice how to communicate in this kind of situation. We can do role-playing, and—"

"I don't want to," Dr. Brown said, vehemently. "She's well-connected in the community, and I'm afraid of what she'd say about me. I can't afford any ill-will."

"You're just going to ignore it?" I said, trying to hide my incredulity. "Dr. Brown, your other team members won't ignore it. They're going to notice. This will affect your practice."

"The best thing is if we just…work on something else," Dr. Brown said. "Systems, maybe. Or profitability."

"So you can just eat the costs of petty theft," I guessed.

She nodded uncomfortably. "It's just easier that way."

The number one thing that keeps my clients avoiding and denying what's going on is *fear*. Here are some common fears:

- "I don't know how to confront that. I don't know how to have those tough conversations."
- "What if there's a big blow up, and someone quits? And then we have turnover—and people still aren't happy!"
- "What if people find out that I'm failing at running my practice?"
- "I thought I was so smart, and I did really well in school, but I don't know how to do this."
- "What if this is all my fault? What does that say about me?"

It's totally normal to feel fear and shame when you're in an uncomfortable situation. You've spent years focusing on being a knowledgeable, capable professional. That's a testament to your brains and work ethic!

But sometimes so many years being professionally graded and quantified can lead us to entrench in a belief that any kind of perceived mistake or failure is a negative statement about our worth, especially if we feel like we're making mistakes in managing our practice.

Acknowledging that things aren't all right in our practice home can be terrifying.

Fear is what makes us avoid discomfort. It makes us close our eyes and pretend not to see problems that are right in front of us. It keeps us locked into tired old patterns that don't serve us, our employees, or our patients. We ignore the things we're afraid of confronting, and we're usually afraid of confronting them because we don't know how.

You can ask yourself: If I can see this, why am I ignoring it? What am I afraid of?

I'm here for you. I've helped people through self-reflection and finding the cracks in the foundation of their practice. If you've seen something broken in your practice home, and you've chosen to ignore it, it's time to use your mirror and get in close.

Using Your Mirror

Now that you're showing up and reflecting on your fears, how are you going to use that to start seeing the systemic issues with your practice home?

When I showed up to my home inspection, I wondered the same thing. How was he going to look in all those hard-to-reach hidden areas that most people forget about until they're broken?

A home inspector uses a mirror to inspect the usually hidden parts of a home—the heat exchange on a furnace, the undersides of siding, the ductwork under a house. It's a terrific tool. In the hands of someone knowledgeable and willicng to apply reflection and light, it can be used to diagnose important issues with a house.

I've been working in dental offices since I was a kid, and chairside since college. When I first saw the home inspector's mirror, I realized it looks a lot like the kind of mirror dentists use to assess teeth.

I can still remember one of the first times I was sitting chairside.

I was thrilled to be assisting my doctor during a procedure, because he was an amazing clinician, and I couldn't wait to learn from him.

I picked up my mirror and took a look—*wow*.

I hadn't expected the patient's condition to look like that! It looked like such a severe problem.

I glanced at Dr. G, wondering if he was as worried and blown away as I felt.

But he didn't seem fazed at all. He picked up his mirror, took a careful look, and then he calmly started explaining to the patient—and to me, the trainee—the diagnosis and the treatment plan.

I remember how impressed I felt that he had the expertise and confidence to dive right in and fix that tooth. It was a great lesson in watching how things that look difficult to me are familiar and doable to those with the skill and will to fix something.

Now, what was the difference between the dentist and me? We were both sitting next to the same patient, but we had totally different perspectives on the same problem.

The patient's problem wasn't the difference. I was afraid of what I saw in the mirror, but the dentist wasn't. It wasn't pretty, it wasn't easy, but he knew it was fixable. He knew what this problem was called, and that helped him know how to fix it.

The difference was the dentist's *training*.

It's normal to be afraid of what we might see. But I'm here with you, and you can do this, and I'll tell you why: your experience with specialty medical care has shifted how you see problems, just like my experience with helping professionals like you has shifted how I see them.

Instead of seeing something insurmountable, you can see something fixable, and the perspectives I share with you here can help create that difference. The problem is the same, but what will have changed is your perspective.

I want to help show you a new perspective, so that you can come to see that the problems in your office are also fixable and learn how to fix them. Sometimes fear keeps us from creating the solutions that are open to us. Once you can view things with resilience and abundance, and not fear and scarcity, new approaches and solutions will appear where before you may have had frustration and shame.

We cannot fix the flaws we *won't* see. So how can we begin seeing the cracks in our foundation?

We need light, and we need to know what we're looking for.

Light in the Mirror: Perfectionism and How It Keeps You in the Dark

I never enjoy finding out that a team member is stealing from the practice, but I'm glad when my inspection turns up such a serious problem, because it's an opportunity to help the doctor or dentist begin to reclaim their professional life.

I arranged a private meeting with the dentist. When we were both sitting, I gathered the evidence, spread the papers on the table, and said, "I'll be blunt. Your office manager is stealing from you."

"I'm not sure how to handle this," the dentist said, looking distraught.

"I'm here to help," I told him. "Unfortunately, I've seen it before. We can start by calling the police and making a statement."

"Yes," the dentist said. Then, he shook his head. "Wait, no. I—if we call the police, then the office will know. And then everyone in town will know, too."

"They don't have to come here," I said, concerned. "We can go to the station."

"No," the dentist said. "I'll just…handle it. Internally."

The dentist ended up letting his office manager go, making her promise to keep the story that she chose to leave to explore other avenues. He didn't want anyone in the office or the community or among his fellow dentists to know what had happened right under his nose. He felt worse about being embarrassed than about being stolen from! That is some powerful perfectionism and shame.

Let's shed some more light on one of the common fears that keeps committed people from showing up: perfectionism.

Perfectionism is the fear-based belief that a person's worth resides in doing everything perfectly. Brené Brown describes it as the "self-destructive and addictive belief system that fuels this primary thought: If I look perfect, and do everything perfectly, I can avoid or minimize the painful feelings of shame, judgement, and blame."

Doctors like the one in the story know there are problems in their practices, but because they don't feel confident in knowing how to address it, they stay silent or try to find something or someone else to blame. They may avoid confronting what wasn't working by ignoring poor systems, by not communicating clearly, or by being authoritarian where they could be authoritative.

Fearing we are ultimately to blame often leads us to hide. We hide by pretending things are fine, even when they aren't. To you, I say: You are not alone. If you are willing to look into the mirror, you can find what you fear, and then you can challenge perfectionism and shame. Self-reflection can become your greatest teacher.

Here are ways to reflect on how perfectionism-based fear may be affecting you.

Don't fear your reflection. Is it hard for you to take feedback or to look too closely at yourself? Don't worry, this is what happens when we're afraid. I understand this deeply—I am a perfectionist myself! There are things I have wanted to do but hesitated in doing or left undone because of my fear. This fear holds all of us back. Sometimes you have to jump and know the pool will have plenty of water.

Examine your expectations. A great way to reflect on your expectations is to write them down. Do you expect to do everything perfectly? Do you expect success on the first try? How many mistakes do you get to make? If you're not open to making lots of mistakes on your way to success, your high expectations may be keeping you in the position of hiding your mistakes.

Shine a light on stress. Do you find yourself avoiding or procrastinating making changes? Does doing anything less than 100 percent feel too risky?

Focus on your strengths. When you think about your mistakes, instead of focusing on failure, ask yourself, "What did I do right?" People who struggle with perfectionism sometimes have a hard time seeing their strengths.

Perfectionism isn't all bad. The traits that lend themselves to people excelling in your profession are only problematic when taken too far. If you recognize yourself in this, then I have good news for you!

We're going to make the shift into something else together: a better foundation for the healthy, happy practice home that's ready to roll with the punches. So let's talk about what fear and perfectionism do to your practice home's foundation, and how to transform it.

Recognizing the Cracks in the Foundation: What's Your Mindset?

First, we're going to work on understanding the difference between scarcity and abundance. Then we'll talk about why it's important for you in rebuilding your practice home and what you can do to begin to make the shift.

A mirror is great at revealing one's mindset. What is mindset? It's the framework around our beliefs, especially our view of our qualities and characteristics. Mindset can define how we approach the world. Mindset influences our self-awareness, our self-esteem, our creativity, our ability to face challenges, our resilience to setbacks, our levels of depression, and our tendency to stereotype, among other things. Much of who we are on a day-to-day basis comes from our mindset, and it can either limit our potential or enable our success.

The scarcity mindset is the zero-sum paradigm of life. In *The 7 Habits of Highly Effective People*, Stephen Covey says, "Most people are deeply scripted in what I call the Scarcity Mentality. They see life as having only so much, as though there were only one pie out there."

People with a scarcity mentality have a very difficult time sharing recognition, credit, power, or profit—even with those who help in the production. They also have a hard time being genuinely happy for the success of others. This mindset comes from the belief that your qualities are carved in stone, that who you are is who you are, period. Intelligence, personality, and creativity are seen as fixed traits, rather than qualities that can be developed.

Scarcity culture asks, "What or who am I supposed to be afraid of?" and "Whose fault is it?" Scarcity mindset tries to find whom to blame.

An abundance mindset comes from the belief that your basic qualities are things you can cultivate through effort. Everyone has different aptitudes, talents, and temperaments, and everyone can also change and grow through experience and application. This abundance mentality flows out of a deep inner sense of personal worth or security. It is the paradigm that there is more than enough to spare for everybody.

This broad, flexible, constantly-expanding foundation makes room for ever more possibilities, options, and alternatives, and it embraces creativity. Willingly practicing this mindset helps you see opportunities and potential in yourself and the people around you. It results in the sharing of prestige, recognition, profits, and decision-making.

This may further help you understand the differences between the two mindsets.

Table 1. Scarcity vs. Abundance Mindset

SCARCITY	ABUNDANCE
Point of View	
Focus is on control—either claiming all of it (bully) or none (victim).	Claiming accountability for what one can change, and working to make that happen.
Physical Energy	
Tense shoulders, clenched jaw, contracted body, uneasy breath.	Rooted, balanced, expansive body; relaxed and alert posture; deep even breath.
Emotional Energy	
Frustration, impatience, anxiety, anger, fear, and helplessness. Gives power to peer pressure, and drains the energy in the room.	Empowerment, engagement, positivity. Connection to productivity or something bigger than yourself and excited by challenges and growth.
Mental Energy	
Confused, narrow, disorganized thinking that focuses on what's not working or justifications of helplessness.	Clear, active, flexible thinking that's able to perceive multiple viewpoints at once and focuses creatively on having many choices and noticing new things.

Listen, working on shifting from scarcity to abundance is hard—I get it. Doing it honestly is tough. I have cheat sheets like these to help me keep working on shifting my mindset. They work as often as I'm willing to use them; I don't use them every day, but I do better on the days that I do.

Mirror as Master Class

Did you recognize yourself in the scarcity column? If you did, then I'm proud of you!

One of the hardest parts of my practice is inviting my professional clients to take a long look in the mirror, but it's also one of the most pivotal, powerful moments in making things better. I know it's not easy to examine ourselves, but it's an important part of being willing to make changes from the foundation up.

This is important to know because, as unhappy as you are now, things can begin to be better now. Things are rough right now for you at work, but instead of seeing this as evidence of failure or an insurmountable problem, you can see that this is a wonderful opportunity.

You can shift into getting creative and open and building new solutions where everyone benefits. In fact, asking "How can we grow?" or "How can we have more fun?" or "How can we succeed more financially?" are all great ways to figure out the best next step for you in your development. This is true whether we're talking about how to find your vision, how to build your team, or how to choose and maintain systems for your unique professional home.

Your mistakes are your apprenticeship, your master class. The smartest thing you can do is to embrace your mistakes and let them become customized professional training. Determining what's gone wrong is a wonderful victory! Let your learning lead to knowledge and then to action. We're going to take your analysis another step and figure out how to use the results.

Laying a New Foundation

My mentor John C. Maxwell says that leaders who have a scarcity foundation pay a high price. "When resources (money, opportunity, recognition) are perceived to be limited, paranoia, fear and politics thrive. In this environment, people become nervous and afraid to make a mistake. As a result, teamwork and innovation suffer. Effective leaders, on the other hand, develop and model an abundance mindset. By doing so, they create an environment where they can positively influence their team—and where their employees can thrive."

Now that we're reflecting on where we've built on scarcity, hopefully you see how important it is to build your practice home on a foundation of abundance. You're here because you're ready for your professional experience to be bigger and better, and the old, fragile foundation can't hold all the good things you're about to create.

The question is: *How do we change our mindset?* How do we move intentionally from never-enough to enough? How do we transform our foundation from something small and brittle, into the expansive, flexible, creative, problem-solving abundance that's going to bring you, your employees, and your patients the better experience you all deserve?

This is the courage to change, and it's a practicable skill. Here are some ways you can start your foundation-transformation process today, right now.

Choose to see opportunity. The next time you see an obstacle in your mirror, flip it around and see the opportunity. Face the challenge with the optimism that surely there's a solution. Make sure your team sees you practicing that attitude. You'll be surprised at how far optimism can go towards helping to resolve problems. Practicing optimism means focusing on the light you can bring into your practice. The more you practice being optimistic, the easier and more reflexive optimism will become.

Remind yourself that there is more than enough. As Covey said, there is enough pie to go around, so break that nasty habit of comparing yourself to others. Repeat after me: There is plenty for everyone. Say the sentence often enough, and it'll become second nature.

Give more of what you want. It might sound crazy, but it really does work: one of the best ways to increase your own abundance is by giving. If you feel scarcity in money, give some to someone less fortunate. If you feel short on time, find a way to spend a little time helping someone in need. Giving has the power to put us in an abundant and appreciative frame of mind.

Spend time in reflection. Take a moment and acknowledge all the positives in your life and work. Gratitude is a powerful aspect of an abundant mindset. A grateful heart is at the center of an abundant life. Everyone gets knocked down sometimes; the grateful can find reasons to get back up.

This is something I struggle with and am still working on. It is hard for me to slow down sometimes and reflect and then be grateful. I heard a dentist speak recently, and she heard an idea I loved: she described to the group how she and her team started a new huddle, where they began every day in gratitude. Isn't that inspiring? Now I try to start each day that way.

Offer words of appreciation. This may be one of the fastest and simplest ways to build a more abundant life, and it costs you nothing! People want to know that their work matters. Let people know how much you value them. Your influence will increase in direct proportion to the appreciation you show your team, and so will your happiness.

Practicing gratitude, appreciation, and self-reflection doesn't have to cost a lot in time or money to have a transformative power in our lives. This is the courage to change, and it's a practicable skill. And, again, you don't need to make grand gestures at the beginning of your process. This is where the word *practice* takes on additional meaning—as you practice these principles, your professional life will improve. Your team will love this, and they need this. Make it a habit to let them know you appreciate them.

You'll know that you are adopting an abundance mindset when opportunities for more learning and success become more readily visible. Once you start to look for more, you will find more. Wayne Dwyer says, "Abundance is not something we acquire, it's something we tune into." Your changing mindset will lead you to see the message in the mess, and your view in the mirror will improve.

The Most Important Thing in the Mirror: You

Remember, as you keep bravely using your mirror, the most important thing is *not* that you get this all at once or that you fix it all right now. We are all a work in progress, and that's great.

The most important thing is that you're still trying.

When you roll with the punches, imperfections and all, not only will you be better able to see and create more creative solutions to your current problems, you also set an amazing and transformative example for your employees, one that tells them that what matters is not their perfection, but their persistence.

Business guru John C. Maxwell calls this the Law of the Mirror. He says, "People do what people see. Reflect on the influence you have on your team. Which mindset do you model? Do you see a positive, abundant mentality reflected in your team leaders? Or are they pessimistic, stingy and competing among themselves for your attention? Remember, you set the tone for your organization."

When we know the goodness of making mistakes and are willing to show up with and for people, with an abundant mind, then we've achieved the first foundational skill in building and maintaining a good practice home. We'll be willing to see the problems because we'll know that we're not alone and that we can successfully address them. It'll really pay off, too, in your professional and personal life.

You'll be able to get in tune with your vision for your practice and mentor your team, and then together you can build an abundantly serene workplace. Once you've taken this journey, you can make room for other people around you to make the same journey too.

It may sound simplistic, but nothing will get better until you commit yourself to be willing to make mistakes and to learn from them, on your way to building a practice home you can be proud of.

Show up, screw up, get up—just don't give up. Things are going to get better, starting with you.

Chapter 2

The Compass Circle of Accountability

Draw Your Circle of Leadership

If you've ever drawn up a blueprint, or done high school geometry, you will recognize this compass.

This compass is a drawing tool that can be used to draw circles. Compasses have two parts, called legs, that are hinged in the middle. One leg has a spike—a sharp, pointy part at its end—and the other part usually has a pencil. They can also be used to measure distances on maps and to help draft blueprints—and that's the function we're going to talk about here.

In order to use a compass to draw a circle, you place the spike where the center of the circle will be, and then you adjust the angle of the pencil leg to shrink or enlarge your circle's size. The narrower the angle of the pencil leg, the smaller your circle will be. If you want to enlarge your circle, you have to move your compass legs apart on its hinge.

Have you ever used a compass with a rusty or sticky hinge? They're difficult to work with, because you have to carefully work to pry them open to the width you need, without hurting yourself on the spike's sharp point. It's not easy, but it's worth doing, because a compass that can draw circles of only one size is not a very useful compass!

I have seen many skilled clinicians without the ability to maintain a business as successful as it should be. In my opinion, practice success centers around leadership. Seek resources to equip yourself to become a strong leader and never stop learning.

–KAREN DAVIS

I meet doctors who are at all different places in their careers. Some are excited and love what they're doing but aren't profitable. Other are profitable but are miserable with their team. And some are living the dream: enjoying what they do while also making a profit.

What's the difference between these practices? The Circle of Accountability.

Circle of Accountability

The circle of accountability begins with you. Your inspiration anchors you in the very center, and that inspiration radiates your vision of who you are and who you want to become. In this circle, you are accountable for showing up and dreaming big and then developing that dream into a plan. It is the *Be* circle.

The second circle is the *Do* circle, and it contains your team and the culture that you'll create with them. Your accountability enters this circle in the form of mentoring your team and ensuring that team members are united around core values. You are accountable for the culture in

Circle of Accountability

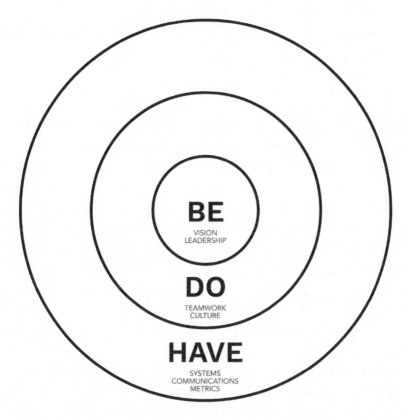

this circle and responsible for making sure that how things are done is aligned with what you believe. In a practice you want to come home to, your team is like your family, and you're responsible for how your practice home is run.

The third circle is the *Have* circle, and it contains tools like systems, metrics, communication, and the experience of the patients you care for. This is your practice's house and all the things you do to put that house in order. You and your team are both accountable in this circle—you must work together and communicate well in order to build and maintain the systems you need, and you are all responsible for creating an amazing experience for the patient.

Leadership is what happens when vision and accountability originate in the middle and radiate outward in expanding circles. Leadership is accountability in action. Accountability is the beginning of leadership. When you're accountable, the first person you lead is you.

Law of the Edge: The difference between two equally talented teams is leadership. A good leader can bring a team to success, provided values, work ethic, and vision are in place.

–JOHN C. MAXWELL

Opening Up the Circle

"I went to dental school, not leadership school! Why can't they just do what I say?"

This is what one doctor said when I started helping her to diagnose and treat the issues in her practice home.

"I went to school to be a dentist," she said. "That's what I should spend my time on, being a dentist. Not the business."

"The business is a really important part," I said. "It takes a lot of work."

"It's their work," she said, meaning her team members. "These systems aren't really that hard, if people just worked! If they were really doing their jobs, then we wouldn't be having these problems." She was firm in the belief that all the issues in her practice were due to her team.

When I meet doctors, it's a lot like when you meet patients with complex cases. I hear things like, "I must be the worst practice you've ever seen!"

Trust me, you're not! I've seen lots of practices with lots of problems. You are far from the only professional with these challenges, and these challenges are fixable.

But one thing that doesn't get easier is when, as a consultant, I have to tell people that part of the problem…is them.

In fact, it's one of the very hardest things I regularly do. It sometimes makes clients feel embarrassed or ashamed. So why do I start from a point that could possibly make a client turn around and walk out the door? I tell the truth, that you are part of the problem, because I know you can be better, and I want you to create the very best practice home you can. Knowing your role in the current problems helps you change course, just like a patient who comes to realize that perhaps part of the problem with their "bad teeth" is the fact that they're living off of soft drinks.

I'm going to help you diagnose and treat the problems keeping your practice from being the best it can be, and the triage process begins with a long look in the mirror.

You'll need to really look honestly at yourself and at how you may be contributing to the drama and dysfunction at work. It may seem hard at first, but it's the magic key to making unmanageable problems manageable.

I know it can be hard to look in the mirror and confront the personal choices there, but the good news is that the same mirror that shows us some of the vulnerable, uncomfortable places we've been can also show us the growing vision of the places we're going.

Push through your shame and discomfort, and commit to the process.

I sensed her lack of accountability and knew it was time to begin triage with one of the hardest questions I have to regularly ask: "What's your role in this?"

"The practice is their responsibility," she said. "They should be running this!"

I paused, and took a deep breath.

"Is this your practice, or their practice?" I asked.

She looked uncomfortable. "Maybe I just need a new team," she said.

I'd met her team. "I'm not sure I agree with that," I said. I had already gotten the sense that the team had a lot of untapped potential that this dentist could access, if she were willing.

"Nobody's perfect," I said. "Your team members are lacking some things—"

The dentist nodded, thinking I was confirming what she had said.

"—but one of the things they're lacking is an accountable leader."

I paused, and the dentist and I sat in the uncomfortable silence as I watched that thought sink in.

"Imagine the expense of replacing all of your employees and retraining every one of them," I said. "What would that do to your practice?"

I could see that the dentist I was helping was uncertain and feeling a lot of emotions. Emotions are a major part of my work—so is truth. I pressed on.

"Even if you replaced everyone and got a totally new team," I said, "you would still need to learn the principles of leadership, or else you're just going to end up right here where we are now."

I've been through this process with clients before, and this wasn't the first time a professional had suggested that they could fix their problems by getting a new team. I know that the first steps a person needs to take to reclaim the power to change their practice for the better, often feel uncertain and arduous.

"Hey, remember, this is about us moving forward past how we've done things," I said, seeing the emotions she was feeling. "It's about showing up."

That emotion can be uncomfortable, but it's what accompanies learning and growth. Powerful change feels vulnerable, but it's worth it.

That's why I commit to helping people like you—I want to give both the truth and plenty of support.

In order to help my client open up a little more towards owning her part in the process, I gave her John C. Maxwell's *21 Laws of Leadership*, so she could see examples of great leadership in action.

After she read it, I could see that the seed had been planted, because the conversations we had took on a different tone. She hung in there and committed to the process. I knew she had caught the vision of the great leader she could be when she started talking about how she was showing up as a leader and which changes could start with her.

When I tell professionals that they're part of the problem, it's because problems don't go away by themselves. And I want your problems to go away! Don't you?

I very much want my clients to begin to enjoy the life they could be having instead of the one they're suffering. I feel so strongly about this that it's my whole mission—to support and guide people just like you in doing what it takes to make their dream practice come true.

If you're having a nightmare experience with your practice, this self-confrontation is a necessary part of taking a practice from a nightmare to your dream.

The best practices are ones where a leader has drawn clear circles of Be, Do, and Have and where that leader has embraced the flow of accountability to begin the transformation that takes them from struggle to success.

When leaders draw their circles small or refuse to draw larger ones, they dwell in scarcity, which brings with it blame and shame. When vision and culture circles are misaligned or when accountability doesn't flow outwards, the result is a poor practice.

When an archer misses the mark, he turns and looks for fault within himself. Failure to hit the bull's-eye is never the fault of the target. To improve your aim, improve yourself.

–GILBERT ARLAND

When leaders prevent themselves from opening their circle, they prevent themselves from reaching a place of influence and joy. They could be so much more than they are now, if only they opened the circle!

That's because the accountability circles are based in abundance. Your success and satisfaction will be as great as the circles you are willing to open and enter.

A More Abundant Leadership

So, now that we've talked about what it looks like to begin the process of opening up, let's see where that process can take you. We started talking about scarcity and abundance in chapter 1. Now, I want to get a little clearer on how working from abundance transforms people into better leaders.

Abundant leaders show up. They show up every day, ready to work and fail forward. Scarcity can lead you to feel shame and to disengage and avoid; abundance will help you keep learning, growing, and improving. The abundance here is in the willingness to fail and get up and try again.

This is one area where I find people have a lot of unlearning to do— they hear "show up" and "work hard", and that translates into needing to look like they know more than they do.

You know what's even braver than maintaining that facade of always being in control and never making a mistake? Showing up as your real self.

Now that takes guts! And it also tells your team that you're committed to growing, learning, and trying hard. Your team will respond powerfully to that, and when you're relieved of the obligation of pretense, you're going to be more comfortable in your professional life and at your practice. That will go a long way to making your practice feel more like a second home.

Abundant leaders have initiative. They take the initiative in problem-solving and growth. They anticipate problems and accept the truth, so that they can take the initiative in making a better future. Scarcity leads someone to deny or avoid problems; abundant leaders take the initiative in solving problems while they're small, before they become undeniable catastrophes.

My mentor John C. Maxwell says that you can measure a leader by the problems they solve—they always look for one their own size.

The courage to be vulnerable is not about winning or losing, it's about the courage to show up when you can't predict or control the outcome.

−BRENÉ BROWN

You can increase your initiative by using your vision to guide you towards what you want more of, and towards action. Take more risks, make more mistakes—successful leaders don't quit; they keep moving and trying again.

Abundant leaders have courage. They're willing to do things that are scary or difficult or new. It can be scary to take stock of where things are or to look at the work ahead.

It can be scary to face the changes and confrontations that you may need to commit to as you proceed through this transformation. Fear is okay, and you don't have to hide it or be ashamed of it. It's a normal part of change.

Remember: it's not courage if you're not scared.

Abundant leaders are generous. This is crucial to true leadership! Your candle loses nothing when it lights another. Leaders want to create success for everyone.

Scarcity can often make work feel like a zero-sum problem, where success can be had only at the expense of others. Scarcity points the finger of blame and refuses accountability. Generosity will accept responsibility and will try to share success with everyone.

You can cultivate this by focusing on gratitude for what you have and then thinking about how you can share that with your team and your patients.

Abundant leaders put others first. Leaders are motivated by true, deep concern for others rather than a desire for convenience or glory.

They ask, "How can I create more value for you?" If you want to get ahead, put others first.

I don't know what your destiny will be, but one thing I know: the only ones among you who will be really happy are those who will have sought and found how to serve.

−ALBERT SCHWEITZER

Walking the Talk

I'm not going to ask you to do anything that I'm not willing to do, so here's a story about a time I needed to shift from scarcity to abundance.

I had just moved into the administrator position at a dental office where I had been working for some time. We had started a new method of presenting financial options to patients. This new process wasn't something I was at all familiar with—I hadn't done any work with the new process, and hadn't expected to need to.

Our office hired a coach to teach us how to use the new system. At our team meeting, the coach wanted to use role-playing to practice—what else—our new financial system, and she wanted me to stand up and role-play this system I didn't know, in front of our whole office.

I had worked hard at being a confident expert, so I thought, "Let's try it. I'll do what I can."

So, we did. The coach and I role-played a situation, and I thought that I did okay, and surely this new system would be a learn-as-you-go thing, right?

Wrong.

The coach said, "Again."

We role-played using the new system again, and I did a little better. Surely I was done.

The coach said, "Again."

What? I looked at her in surprise.

I could see my teammates were surprised, too.

I gritted my teeth and tried again. And again. And again.

By the time we finished role-playing a fourth time, I was sweating bullets. I was definitely done—but then the coach began critiquing me again.

I just couldn't take it anymore.

I said, shaken, "This is unbelievable. I clearly can't do this. Forget it. I guess I quit."

And then I got up and walked out of the room.

I was in the hall, still trying to pull myself together, when one of my office friends came and found me.

"I can't do this," I told her. "I cannot do this."

"Angela," my friend said, "Don't take the critique to mean that you're not doing well."

I was still angry and upset, but I was also listening.

"You do this better than any of us," my friend continued. "Now, get back in there, and show her that you can do it!"

I took a breath and dug deep. Really deep!

I thought, "Okay. I'm not giving up. I'm going to go in there, and I am going to bring my good attitude, and I am going to nail this sucker, so I never have to do it again!"

And I did. I went in there determined to try again and succeed, and I nailed that sucker. The coach said, "Now, that's what I'm talking about! That's what I want you to do every time."

I began using this process with real patients during office hours, using the steps and verbiage that the coach had drilled into me. Two things happened.

First, once I started putting the training to work, I began to understand why the coach had emphasized what she had and why she'd repeatedly drilled me on this process.

Second, I began to have some amazing success! This new process was a game-changer for encouraging case acceptance with patients.

I was so glad I'd dug deep and persevered through my discomfort. That discomfort was the feeling of me going to the next level in being able to do my job, and I was so much the better for it.

Are You Ready to Widen Your Circle?

Open yourself up and draw that circle a little wider, so you can move closer to giving yourself and your practice that gift of leadership.

As you are willing to move from small scarcity-based circles to wider abundance-based circles, you will transform and then be able to mentor your team through the same transformation.

When placed correctly, these circles provide a wonderful experience from the leader to the patient, enlarge everyone's capacity for a better life at work and at home, and put goodness into the world that wasn't there before. They make your practice and your work more valuable, because they provide more value.

Once you lean more abundantly into the leadership role, that magical transformation begins, and I love that moment!

The best practices are vision-centered places where professionals lead teams united in a culture based on excellent core values, supported by systems and communication, in order to provide an amazing experience for patients.

Great practices don't just happen—they're built by people like you, who are deliberate about creating greatness.

Great practices come from great leaders, and you are going to be that great leader.

Now *that* is the kind of practice you can really come home to.

I'll be honest with you. This wider circle will increase the number of things you are accountable for, and the opening up may be a little uncomfortable. It takes work to open up, and this is where your willingness to show up and fail forward works powerfully on your future's behalf. Discomfort is what growing feels like.

Do you want more? Be more.

Want more success? Draw your circle larger.

Change hinges on you.

I'm here for you, and I know you can do this.

If you can become the leader you ought to be on the inside, you will be able to become the person you want on the outside. People will want to follow you. And when that happens, you'll be able to tackle anything in this world.

–JOHN C. MAXWELL

Chapter 3

Building Your Blueprint

You Are the Architect of Your New Future

You've shown up to your home inspection, ready to look at yourself and your foundation in the mirror, ready to rebuild your foundation from scarcity to abundance. You've got your compass circle, ready to draw. Now you're ready for the next step in building a business you can come home to: your blueprint.

Have you ever been in a house that seemed really nice but was somehow wrong? Have you ever walked into an entryway that was elaborate and huge, full of unusable space, that connected to a cramped living room? Have you struggled with a game room too small to contain the pool table it was meant to hold, or rooms with easy-stain carpeting and tile that shattered all of your dishes?

If you've ever experienced the frustration of a poorly placed light switch, inadequate closet space, or a kitchen with a dishwasher that blocked traffic when it was open, then you know the everyday cost of poor design.

In your practice, these are all issues that will eventually be fixed on the contractor level—and we'll talk about how to, later in this book—but these issues all need to be fixed on the architect level first.

Every successful build begins with a clear design. If you've ever hired an architect to help with building or remodeling a home, then you know the difference between a contractor and an architect.

All things are created twice. There's a mental or first creation, and a physical or second creation to all things. Take the construction of a home, for example. You create it in every detail before you ever hammer the first nail into place ... Then you reduce it to blueprint and develop construction plans ... You have to make sure that the blueprint, the first creation, is really what you want, that you've thought everything through. Then you put it into bricks and mortar... You begin with the end in mind. Through imagination, we can visualize the uncreated worlds of potential that lie within us.

–STEPHEN COVEY

Architect or Contractor?

Architects are trained in building design, engineering, and ergonomics. At the beginning of a major project, the architect's job is to examine your site or current house, listen to your dreams and needs, and then create a beautiful, customized vision that will solve the problems you're currently living in.

Contractors are terrific at gathering resources and engineering efficient and logical solutions to problems. They are key to directing teams in building workable structures out of available materials—but they cannot do their job unless an architect has already done theirs.

A contractor without a vision has no way to prioritize their resources. They can't buy lumber or direct builders until they know what they need and where it needs to be placed. Without a blueprint, a contractor cannot fulfill their potential.

Up till now, you've probably been thinking like a contractor. Maybe you hoped that if you showed up and worked hard at using your skills, putting together a team, and building a practice, then your hard work and good intentions would create a practice you could come home to.

But by now you've seen that that's just not the case. It's not that you didn't work hard; it's not that you're incapable; it's not that you haven't tried; you just didn't have the right blueprint for your needs.

Those of us who aren't trained to read blueprints may sometimes have a hard time visualizing the difference that details on a blueprint can make to a finished home. But we all have a gut-level understanding of home design. When we experience the details of thoughtless blueprints, we know it. We know when a home hasn't been designed with us in mind.

We know, deep within, when it's not working.

Fortunately, the solution we need also comes from deep within: our vision. Your vision will determine what you want to be, do, and have.

In this chapter, I'm going to help you be your own architect. I'm going to guide you through brainstorming your own dreams and how to turn those dreams into plans. I'll give you questions that will help you discern your own vision, customized to your personal foundation, ready to support your unique needs and dreams, so you'll be ready to lead a team of builders in making your vision a reality.

Your Mission—Should You Choose to Accept It

A first meeting with an architect often consists of going over pictures and floor plans of different homes, so that you and your architect can better pinpoint what kind of home you love, and what doesn't work for you.

It takes some time to go through pictures together, but a lot of clients find it deeply enjoyable to discover a way to articulate their ideals and their desires.

Naming what you need brings you a step closer to being able to create your dream. Seeing what we want to live in action helps us recreate it for ourselves.

This process is part self-discovery and part self-creation. Set aside time to meet with your inner architect and have a long talk about where you live, and what you'd like it to be. Respect the process.

I'm a believer in dreaming big and having fun with this part of the process. It's one of my favorite things to support a client in, and I'm going to be here for you as I walk you through these questions now.

So are you ready to have a meeting with your architect? You're invited to a nice relaxing brainstorming meeting where you can get to know yourself and your dreams. The designs you're going to look over and think about are the people who have succeeded.

Blueprints are on paper; go ahead and feel free to grab a notebook, so you can jot down your thoughts during this process.

Vision is everything for a leader. It leads the leader. It paints the target. It sparks and fuels the fire within, and draws him forward. It is also the fire lighter for the others who follow that leader.

–JOHN C. MAXWELL

Who Do You Admire?

A solid vision statement has a long-range view, focuses on the future, and is a source of inspiration. We're going to use what inspires you to help you inspire others!

So, to begin, think of someone highly influential in your life. It could be a teacher, colleague, family member, or a friend—pick someone who's powerfully affected your life. Do you have their name and face in mind? Good.

Ask yourself what you admire most about them. What is it about them that makes you grateful for them? What do you appreciate? What about them makes you wish you were like them?

Now—because self-recognition is so important—ask yourself what qualities you've gained from them or would like to gain.

Again, this is a dream-big thing. It's not about beating yourself up! The goal in this entire process is to create a safe environment in which to fail and move forward.

Just relax, and with gratitude to this inspiring, influential person, consider where you've succeeded in being like them and where you still have room to succeed in being more like them.

Becoming Your Version of Your Hero

"Let's start with who your inspiration is," I told Dr. Jensen. I love the positive energy clients have when they focus on who inspires them, and it helps us to work together on showing up and making their future match their inspiration.

This time, though, we had an interesting challenge.

"Oh, definitely Dr. Greg," she said. "He's my mentor. I'd love to make more of what he had."

"Tell me about Dr. Greg," I said.

As Dr. Jensen told me about Dr. Greg, it became clear why he was an inspiring figure. Greg was her previous boss, a massively successful dentist beloved both in the office and in their community. He was a people-oriented leader who was generous and abundant and positive, and who naturally communicated positivity and affection. He had a reputation for seeing the potential in people and patiently investing in them as their potential became realized.

Naturally, people adored him, including my client, Dr. Jensen, who'd been a beneficiary of his kindness herself. He'd established an amazing practice with a full schedule of longtime patients, a tightly-knit team, and a place in the community. It was the kind of practice I love to see, and when my client had purchased Dr. Greg's practice after his retirement, she'd inherited it all: the patients, the team, the reputation—and a new problem.

"This all sounds amazing," I said. "I can see why you admire him."

"I do," my client said. "I admire Dr. Greg, and I'd love to be a wonderful dentist and leader. But I'm not able to do what he did!"

She told me how she'd been struggling in his shadow. She described how she'd begun to have problems with her team at work and that the rapport she'd enjoyed when Dr. Greg was at the helm had started breaking down.

"I'm trying to do what he did, how he did it," she said. "I love his legacy and I want to preserve it. But it's coming apart. I can't do it."

"I can tell this is hard for you, and you're doing a great job showing up and being honest," I told her. "Usually when we find someone who inspires us, especially in our professional field, our goal is to have what they've had, by doing what they have done, and that can start with trying to be as they've been. But—"

"—But I'm not him," she concluded glumly.

"That's true," I said. "You're not Dr. Greg. And that's not a bad thing."

"My team's falling apart," she said. "He created such a great practice, and now people are so unhappy. I don't know how to do what he did to help make everyone happy."

"You're an excellent dentist and a really nice person," I told her. "But you aren't Dr. Greg. You're more quiet and reserved, which is not a bad thing. It's just that your team is used to Dr. Greg's style of communication and leadership, and I think you're still figuring out your own."

So now that she was willing to show up as her naturally reserved, quiet self, I could start helping her figure out her Be, Do, and Have.

Good job! We're getting there. Here's the next step.

Who Do You Want to Be?

With your influential person in mind, and their admirable qualities, ask yourself: What would I like to *Be*?

Maybe your influential person is known for their generosity or grit. Which of their qualities would you like to have? What character strengths would you like to develop?

What do you think that would look and feel like, to have those qualities? How would you use them?

Begin this statement with "I believe..." or "I have a vision of a world..."

This part of your vision is about your inner purpose, the cause on a level higher than business. Business is very important—we wouldn't be doing this if we didn't believe that—but this step is about the world you want to help make. Southwest Airlines' mission statement doesn't say anything about being an airline. Instead, it says:

> *"The mission of Southwest Airlines is dedication to the highest quality of Customer Service delivered with a sense of warmth, friendliness, individual pride, and Company Spirit. We are committed to provide our Employees a stable work environment with equal opportunity for learning and personal growth."*

Your mission isn't about *what* you do, it's about *why* you want to do what you do. What is the world you want to help make?

Remember, now's the time to get messy and take the time your process needs. You may need to write a lot of statements before you find the ones that sound just right—and you may be surprised by what you discover about yourself! These discoveries are wonderful moments. Savor them.

When you find the one or two "I believe" lines that you feel best represent your inner, higher purpose, then ask the next question.

A mission statement is not something you write overnight... But fundamentally, your mission statement becomes your constitution, the solid expression of your vision and values. It becomes the criterion by which you measure everything else in your life.

Writing or reviewing a mission statement changes you because it forces you to think through your priorities deeply, carefully, and to align your behavior with your beliefs.

—STEPHEN COVEY

Here's a home blueprint example: "We envision a welcoming home where family enjoys spending time together." This is about why we need a home and what we're hoping to have happen there.

What Do You Want to Do?

Once you know your *why*, it's time to think about the way you want to realize your vision.

What do you hope to accomplish? What kind of contributions do you want to make? You've already articulated why you do what you do; it's time to explain how you'll do it.

Think of two to five distinct characteristics or values about you and your practice that make you unique. Lots of people can want to change the world; where it gets interesting is how they, personally, are going to do it, with their unique set of abilities and interests.

As you brainstorm, feel free to start off vague, but your goal here is to get as concrete and specific as possible. For your vision to be actionable later, it needs to be specific now.

If this were a blueprint for a home that embodies the vision of "We envision a welcoming home, and a family that loves to spend time together," then this is where you specify what makes your home distinctly welcoming. Maybe it's a spacious kitchen where people can cook and eat together comfortably.

For instance, saying "We want to be innovative" sounds really nice, but it's not as clear as it could be. Instead, you can narrow it down to "We create multiple solutions."

When I help clients with this portion of their vision discernment, I like to remind them about how leaders and world-changers are focused on how they can serve others. Often, focusing on how to help others and change their lives will help us see what our most fulfilling contribution may be.

For professionals with your level of training, that can include a focus on the patient. How can you bring wellness and healing to others?

If this were a blueprint for a home, we could begin with the Be—"We envision a welcoming home for a family that loves to spend time together"—and brainstorm some general ideas for Do: What kind of welcoming and enjoyment will the home offer? We can make food, sit outside, and watch movies.

These are great ideas of the things we'd want to do in our unique home, but in order to create a better blueprint, we need to get more specific. So, maybe after some more brainstorming, we figure out that "Make food" will become "Bake artisanal sourdough together." "Sitting outside" in more specific terms could be "We want to entertain people outside three seasons of the year." "Watch movies" could become "We enjoy weekly movies together in a comfortable home theater."

What Do You Want to Have?

Now we're going to outline your specific goals.

What kind of results do you want? What services do you offer? What money or possessions or markers of financial success and security do you want to have? For a lot of my clients, this list can be the longest and sometimes the most quickly filled out.

That's great—when we have more, we can give more, and part of the point of this is personal financial stability. A practice that's taking business and vision to the next level has more to offer and should bring in more money as well.

It's important to keep in mind, however, that power, influence, and lasting satisfaction are going to be found in your Bes, not only your Haves. The Haves are there to support your Be. Get specific on your goals, so that you can better embody your Be.

So, finishing your home blueprint, let's lay it out. We know why we need this home—a place that we can come together in and enjoy—and the special things we'll do there—baking and entertaining. With this step, we will specify the what, the goals, that will embody those distinct things.

Be: We envision a welcoming home for a family that loves to spend time together.

Do and *Have*: We enjoy time together by baking artisanal bread, which means the kitchen will need to be open and spacious, with a proofer and oven and nearby dining. We will entertain outside on a patio, with a pergola and comfortable furniture on easy-to-clean surfaces. We will enjoy weekly movies in our home theater, with built-in surround sound and comfortable seating for everyone, including guests.

Do you see how we went from the Be to the Do and Have? If you told an architect that you wanted a nice-looking home where you could enjoy dinner with your family and watch movies, you could end up with a number of homes that wouldn't fulfill your needs.

But if you can tell your architect that you need a mid-century-modern home with a spacious kitchen designed for baking, a well-appointed and easy-to-clean patio for entertaining, and a large home theater that can hold several pieces of furniture, then that architect will be able to design a home that matches your vision of something you can truly come home to. A blueprint begins with an idea and ends with exact measurements.

Here's another example of the magic of specificity:

Be: We want to change the world by making people happier and more confident. We want to increase joy.

This practice begins with people who want to bring joy to the world. Isn't that fantastic? I find that some of the most inspiring Bes are based in this kind of servant leadership. This practice found inspiration in heroes who focused on helping others.

Do: We are especially well-trained and adept at keeping up with the latest techniques. We want to be known for making our patients feel special and comfortable and for caring about their health.

The partners working here realized that with their specific set of abilities with technology and a focus on creating dazzling smiles, that their focus needed to move away from general dentistry to specialize in cosmetic dentistry. That's great! Already this mission statement was helping them to realize the shifts they needed to make to align their work with their vision.

Have: We need high-quality materials, the latest technology, lots of adept team members, and all the details that make patients look forward to coming to our office, like heated massage chairs and other comfort items.

Once they realized they needed to specialize in cosmetic dentistry, they thought about what was most important to carrying out that mission so that they could meet and exceed expectations.

The finished mission statement:

> *We are the leading team in cosmetic dentistry today. We are a group of three dedicated individuals who share the common ideal of being genuinely concerned with your overall health and self-esteem. We will provide you with a dazzling smile using the finest materials, the very latest in cutting-edge technology, and the most advanced skills and services. You will receive a truly remarkable, relaxing experience while we focus on your comfort.*

They went from their initial dream to how they were going to carry it out. Can you see how a big dream—"create joy"—went from big and abstract to very concrete and specific? I bet as you read this mission statement, you can even easily imagine what kinds of equipment they use and what their office looks like. That's the magic of specificity.

Bringing the Mission Statement to Life

"I love how Dr. Greg loved people, but I'm just not like that," my client said. "I don't just walk up to people and hug them."

"That's okay," I said. "We're going to work on building your practice leadership in a way that is totally your own. Let's talk about what problems you're seeing, and then we'll brainstorm together about some possible solutions."

Dr. Jensen described her team's faltering communication. I'd met them, and I knew they were a solid team, but used to a more hands-on, effusive, praise-laden style than Dr. Jensen naturally tended towards.

"We know that your communication style isn't just like his," I said. "And, again, that's not bad. But your team is experiencing this change as a loss, and because you're still figuring out your communication style, there's a gap there, full of the unknown. Which is scary for them."

"What's the fix?" she asked. "What can I do to connect with them and reassure them?"

I really liked how Dr. Jensen focused on what she could do to show up for her team. I can brainstorm lots of possible approaches and solutions with professionals, but no idea can work without the professional's willingness.

By focusing on putting her team first, Dr. Jensen was already inhabiting that inspirational place that she'd defined by her mentor's people-centered leadership. By being willing to show up, she was already beginning to define her own unique style of leadership. This was crucial; in order for our brainstormed solutions to work, Dr. Jensen first needed to show up as herself, as the fully wonderful person she was, instead of seeing herself as a failed or lesser version of her mentor.

After we centered her in her own individual Be, we started talking honestly about her Do and discovered that part of her team's disaffection was likely due to her different communication style. She tended to be more reserved, and when she did talk to her team, it was to quietly point out an area where they'd done something wrong. That kind of correction is part of being a leader, but Dr. Greg had cushioned his corrections in connection, and his team was used to his very open communication style and signature ratio of praise to instruction.

"You're strong at details and follow-through," I said. "Let's build on that."

Dr. Jensen and I talked about how crucial it is for people to feel appreciated, and that this principle would build a foundation for her own developing leadership style.

We agreed she wasn't going to hug people—that's an important personal comfort thing that needs to be done carefully in a professional setting—but she could use words to reassure and direct her team. We brainstormed some concrete strategies that would help her adjust her communication style.

"Words matter," I told her. "They go a long way to connect to your team. Start by making sure you say 'good morning' when you get to the office, and say 'goodbye' before you leave."

"That sounds really simple," Dr. Jensen said. "That's going to fix my communication problem with my team?"

"These small, simple things, done well every day, lay a foundation for bigger and better communication," I told her. "It shows you notice them and care. And then we'll build on it. Get five coins and put them in your right pocket. Every time you compliment your team members on something they've done well, you move a coin to your left pocket."

"Five a day, every day?" Dr. Jensen asked.

"Every day," I confirmed. "I know it sounds simple, but it's a real shift in mindset. When you follow through on the details of these small, simple things, you can change your perspective and train yourself to both look for the good and also praise people for it."

"Let's give it a try!" she said.

Dr. Jensen practiced connecting with her team and looking for the good as she settled into her new role as her practice's leader. After a while, she discovered that she also enjoyed and was terrific at giving gifts to her team members, because that show of appreciation suited her quiet, reserved, detail-oriented style. She did great at being like her inspiration, Dr. Greg, but living up to that in her own unique way.

A personal mission statement has the power to give you guidance in your life and powerfully affect you and your business for the better. Now that you've got a values-based blueprint for yourself, you're ready to take the lead in creating a vision-based culture and build your team of builders.

Chapter 4

Building Your Builders

Use Vision to Change Your Company Culture and Create Your Team

You've shown up for your home inspection and gotten brave with your mirror; you've grasped your compass and used your inspiration to draw a visionary plan for what you want your practice to be.

That vision you have for the future is where you anchor the fixed spike of your compass. Using this, you can draw your possibilities within the circle of one central inspiration. This is your first circle of accountability.

So, now that you've got your legs under you, and your spike is dug in deep to your vision of the future you could have, we're going to open a little wider so you can extend your circle of influence. Then we're going to take that blueprint and get ready to rebuild your practice.

We're going to talk about how to take your vision—your *Be*—and mentor your team into creating a visionary culture of *Do*.

We'll talk about why and how you need to invest in building your best team of builders; we'll talk about the differences between vision and culture; and we'll talk about how you can build a visionary culture with your team.

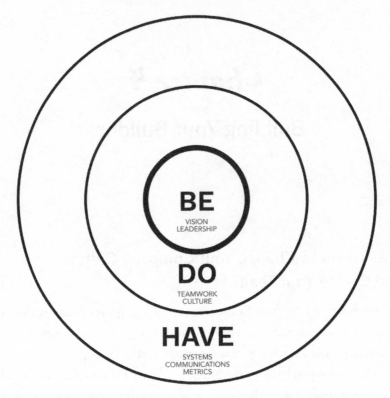

Circle of Accountability

But you can't do this alone—you need a team to help you enlarge this circle. So let's talk about why and how to build the builders who will bring your vision to life—because if you want a practice you can come home to, you need to treat your team like family.

Culture Eats Vision for Lunch

Now that you've got a visionary blueprint for what you want your practice to become, it's time to use your mirror to see where your blueprint doesn't match with your current practice. There's going to be a gap, but your visionary leadership is the key to creating an intentionally abundant, joyful culture that will build up the team of builders who will close that gap between where your practice is now and where you'd love it to be.

When I work with doctors and dentists on vision, I also spend time working on the core beliefs of the team so that we can create a culture that will be properly mindful of the vision. I've noticed that the teams that do best at this culture creation are those who agree to a set of core values and who transmit those core values to new hires.

You see, you can articulate a terrific, clear vision to your team, but without a supportive culture in place, you'll never achieve that vision. Like families, every practice has its own culture.

You've got a culture already! The big question is: Is it the culture you want? Is your practice's current culture serving everyone as well as it should?

If your culture is built on scarcity, blame, or conflict avoidance, then it's not going to be able to help you rebuild your practice. Building your vision means working on culture—like John C. Maxwell says, "Culture will eat Vision for lunch!"

Vision is about *someday*, and culture happens every day. You and your team need to think about both the future and also the present—not only where you're going but also how you're going to get there.

A leader is one who knows the way, goes the way, and shows the way.

–JOHN C. MAXWELL

A good vision should improve your whole life and make your professional and personal lives better. Vision says, "This is what we do"; culture says, "And this is how we do it."

It's your job to help your team figure out what everyone needs to do and how to do it every day, so you can get to the future where your vision becomes reality.

The opposite is true, too—a practice with a wonderful culture but no vision is probably a really nice place to visit, but it's not going to have the impact it could if it was galvanized by a new vision. You need both vision and culture.

Vision can't be demonstrated because it's a belief. It's not yet a reality. But culture can be lived by example, and it needs to be, beginning with you and including everyone in your practice.

A leader and team need to act every day in a way that builds the vision into the culture. This is the only way to build your blueprint: through everyday work as a team.

Only with both vision and culture can you move forward to create the systems you need to support your new, expansive, successful culture, the kind that helps you and your team every day and provides your patients with incredible professional care.

Law of Identity: Shared values define the team. The type of values you choose for the team will attract the type of members you need. Values give the team a unique identity to its members, potential recruits, clients, and the public. Values must be consistently stated and restated, practiced, and institutionalized.

–JOHN C. MAXWELL

Trouble at Home

"It's like a family reunion in here—and not the good kind! I'm so tired of my team!"

Team problems had brought me to this practice in the South. There's a beautiful culture of hospitality there, but unfortunately this practice had dropped the ball on creating that hospitality for each other and, because of this, had none to offer their patients.

The dentist described the punch list of problems to me: This team member wasn't making phone calls. That team member wasn't diagnosing anything. The hygienist wasn't discussing treatment enough with the patients. The team wasn't asking patients about referrals for orthodontics or implants.

This dentist was solid on his vision for a welcoming, patient-centered practice that was financially successful. He had done great work looking inward and anchoring his vision in inspiration—but his team and his practice's culture wasn't following suit.

He described to me how his team wasn't filling his schedule with enough appointments or offering financial options to the patients who needed them. There was little accountability, and the culture of his practice had become one of finger-pointing and hostility. Everyone was on edge.

This dentist's breaking point—and what led him to call in my help—was when two back-office team members were so unprofessionally unkind to each other during an appointment that a long-time, valued patient had become understandably distressed by this inhospitable environment. She had decided to end their relationship and begin going to another dentist.

"I always have to keep them apart, just like cousins who fight at a family reunion," he told me. "We're all walking on eggshells!"

"That tension sounds so uncomfortable," I said. "I'm not surprised your patient picked up on that and left."

The dentist nodded, looking angry and sad. "And I blame myself, because maybe I could have been there to stop them from fighting or to make amends to the patient, but—ironically—I was too busy dealing with the chaos from my other team members."

He took a deep breath and continued. "I got into dentistry so I could be financially stable, and of course I need to fix that," he said. "But, more importantly, I got into this because I wanted to help people. I'm so upset that my practice actually drove someone away!"

He paused. "Sometimes I wonder if I'd be better off just working this practice alone."

This practice's team was far from the committed family culture that the best professional practices maintain; there were team members that fought so much that the dentist had to spend valuable time and energy maintaining them in separate schedules.

This isn't the first time I've seen a loss of trust drive a wedge between members of the work family in a practice, or heard a dentist or doctor express fearful frustration about the state of their practice.

"I'm really glad you called me," I told him. "I've seen this before, and I can help you. I know you're upset with your team right now. Part of why you're upset is because your practice hasn't been working as it should. The vision you have both for taking care of patients and for your financial success can't be accomplished without having people; I'm going to help you make things better by investing in your team."

Somehow we've come to equate success with not needing anyone. Many of us are willing to extend a helping hand, but we're very reluctant to reach out for help when we need it ourselves. It's as though we've divided the world into 'those who offer help' and 'those who need help'. The truth is that we are both.

—BRENÉ BROWN

Making Good for Your Team of Investors

If you've been practicing for a while, you've already met the professional's paradox: You need a team precisely because only you have the accreditation to offer specialty care. Becoming a clinician with your level of education and accreditation has been a task that's required not only your devotion but also the investment and work of your instructors, mentors, and supporters.

A smoothly running professional practice that fulfills its potential in caring for people is too large a task for just one person, and, that's what brings most of us to this point of practice home renovation in the first place. Our work family isn't working, and it's keeping everyone from being the best they can be.

Part of what brought you to this point was the frustration of not being able to use those hard-earned clinical skills to do what only you can do. Instead, you're spending time and energy on tasks that you ought to be able to delegate.

You can't reach out *to* help until you reach out *for* help. After all, you didn't get here alone, and you won't be able to continue alone.

In order to make those investments by multiple people who've believed in you along the way come to fruition and in order to give the quality of care that you want and maintain the financial and organizational soundness you intend, you're going to need another supportive team of people willing to invest in you to help you and the patients who need your skills. You're going to need a functional work family.

It's up to you to decide if you want to spend time putting out fires and repairing damage or if you'd rather invest in quality fireproofing that you can confidently and serenely maintain on a regular basis.

But one thing is clear: You are going to invest time, energy, and resources in these issues, either way. You're either going to be reacting to team issues while struggling, or you can joyfully invest in your team in a planned and nurturing way. And until you invest in leading your team, you can't make good on your many investments in yourself. They're what make your vision a reality.

So let's talk about how a professional like you can invest in your team of investors and lead with gratitude for the people who are willing to commit their work lives to supporting you in your practice.

The First Rule of Culture Club Is Everybody Should Talk About Culture Club

First, a note on team training.

The goal here is to create a safe environment in which your teams can fail forward. I find that keeping things fun and nurturing and including the whole team in the process is the best way to help people open up to change.

This is why I start all my training with embracing failure and praising people who show up, no matter how many mistakes they've made. I try to help leaders like you internalize this nurturing, encouraging, energizing, abundance-based view of growth, so that you can also offer that same abundance to your teams, by inviting their participation.

Remember, if you want a work team that operates like a fantastic family, you need to treat them like family. As a doctor or dentist owning and running a practice, remember that the first people you take care of are your own.

Begin with praise. Offer support and training, and model what showing up looks like. Building is beautiful! Find something successful and build on it. Start working on what you can; you can come back for the rest.

If you want to reach your potential or strive for the seemingly impossible, you need to be a team player. It may be a cliché, but it is nonetheless true: individuals play the game, but teams win championships.

–JOHN C. MAXWELL

Take the lead in creating a culture that says, "We are a family, and we want everyone to have the opportunity to be successful. We can have training and have fun with learning new things."

This step in the process is a great time to connect. People know when they're really valued and supported, and they will want to show up for someone who sees the good in them. That's the kind of leadership that matters most.

The Team Compass: Finding Yourselves, One Direction at a Time

Human beings are built to be moral. We are social creatures, and sharing a moral vision as a group builds us a culture based in dignity and well-being.

My business mentor John C. Maxwell describes a compass made of these parts: moral (looking above); intuitive (looking within); historical (looking behind); directional (looking ahead); and strategic (looking around).

Here's how these compass points look in your practice.

A Moral Compass: Look Above

Our team was growing very quickly; the practice had gone from one doctor and three team members to three doctors and seventeen team members. Adding more team members and having more success was wonderful, but it came with a challenge: how do we keep our culture intact?

In order to work on bringing integrity to the vision, we did a values exercise as a team. First, we asked everyone to list their top ten values. Then we got out a white board and wrote down the ideas people shared, so that we could discuss them.

One of the values we discussed was the value of *time*. We discussed what our practice's definition of "on time" meant. Does it mean exactly on time? Is five minutes late still "on time"? Or, when we say "on time", do we really mean "fifteen minutes early"? If we tell the team we need them there on time at 7:45, when will they be there?

It's very important to define what these values look like in detailed, concrete terms, so that the whole practice agrees to the same definition.

That's the foundation of a shared moral compass: the values that we agree are important.

We went through and defined each value that people had listed and worked out the details as a team. We worked on what values like "taking care of patients" or "supporting each other" looked like in practice and wrote them down and agreed to each as a group.

We kept all that in writing, not only to remind ourselves about what mattered most to us as a practice team but also to help us with interviews for the new hires we were making. We would go over our values and definitions with each hire, telling them that these are our values in our practice, and we'd ask each one if these values were something they could agree to and uphold while working with us. It became a great way to see which potential hires were aligned with us and which ones we could wish well and send on their way.

Teams that create a moral compass together are the ones that move in the right direction.

An Intuitive Compass: Look Within

I love helping practice owners and office managers look within and develop their intuitive compasses in order to become leaders who can direct great teams. Leaders like you need to know which direction feels right, so that you can set goals in that direction, while lighting a fire under the people you're leading. That intuitive fire is what will make you and your team unstoppable, and it's why many winning leaders have a mentality of "If you can't play at our level, you can't play on our team."

As you hone your leadership intuition, you'll be able to sense your people's red flags that signal a need for more of your attention and caution, and you will sense how to best motivate the people you're investing in. The most important goals can't be done alone, and when you continually look within to calibrate your intuitive compass, you'll be better able to look within others as well, so that you can work together in the right direction towards those common goals.

Law of the compass—a team that embraces a vision becomes focused, energized, and confident. It knows where it's headed and why it's going there.

–JOHN C. MAXWELL

A Historical Compass: Look Behind

Nearly everyone gets excited and motivated when they see their own growth. Building a historical compass through sharing stories about where leaders and teams have been is a great way to encourage teams to keep moving forward. It works because once you and your team know that you've already accomplished amazing change, you feel even better about taking on the next challenge.

One story that I've seen motivate teams in growing practices was when a leader said, "Hey, do you remember when we were first building our practice and we didn't have digital photography or X-rays? Remember how we were able to grow and be productive, and also we felt that learning that new technology was a major challenge? Do you remember how we took on the challenge of learning new skills and processes and tech, and how great it felt to conquer those skills together and to see our practice grow even more? Let's take that ability we know we have and learn some new skills together and figure out how to teach our new hires, so that our practice can go to the next level."

To build a historical compass, find examples of things that your practice has done that worked well and things that didn't. Then ask yourself and your team these questions: What didn't work, and how can we steer away from that? What did work, and how can we get closer to that? Before taking on each new challenge, take a moment to remind your team that, just like before, you and your team will start right where you're at and will take things to the next level together.

A Directional Compass: Look Ahead

Helping leaders create a directional compass is one of the best parts of my work, because not only do I get to work on dream-building with leaders but I also get to teach them how to include their team in that.

Dream building and vision board work are processes that build tremendous positive energy in leaders and teams. That's the kind of energy that connects teams to leaders and builds momentum. I love watching this happen, and here's how I do it.

First, begin by knowing that there are no wrong answers. Throw every idea out there. This process works best when people are relaxed and positive.

Next, think about what you like the most. If you could have your ideal day, schedule, doctor, or employee, what would that look like? What are the characteristics of those things? What are the details?

As you name your ideals in detail, you lay the groundwork for the next step: putting goals in place and breaking each goal down into individual steps and responsibilities for each individual.

Remember, building a directional compass is an inherently positive process. This work is meant to lead somewhere! Make sure there's a destination that you've named and that it has a celebration attached. If the goal is to create so much success together that the practice can afford to move into a new, bigger building, make sure you mark that occasion with a practice trip to the beach. Build and maintain positivity by recognizing and celebrating achievements. It's a wonderful way to maintain the dream energy that fuels your directional compass.

A Strategic Compass: Look Around

I love the big, expansive fun of dream building, but those dreams can't come to pass without building a strategic compass. This is the area where a lot of people fall short, and the key to building strategy is tracking your metrics. You can't have a strategy without data.

Build your strategic compass first by breaking down the tasks to reach the goals your exercise of ideals revealed. Get specific on timeline and what incremental success will look like. Where do you and your team need to be in three months, six months, and a year from now? What kinds of strengths and skills do leaders and teams need to build to get the whole practice there, and what will those strengths and skills look like? How will you measure that progress?

Now is the time to figure that out, and here's why: growth processes don't always happen exactly according to plan. That's ok! We don't need to have a perfect plan to get started. But the problem I see happening is that people get frustrated with the whole process because they're not seeing improvement in one area, and so they change the goal.

Don't change the goal; change the system you're using, and adjust course with that system to keep working towards your goal. If your trackers are indicating an issue, then use your directional compass as a baseline on which to build flexibility. Ask: is there a different way we could do this? Do we need different training? Do we need to give someone else a given task?

You already know, through your dream-building that the goal is worth having, and defining metrics at the beginning of the process will help you track your progress and will guide you in how to adjust systems so that you can maintain your course. Stay aware, stay flexible, tweak things, and then give your new systems enough time to prove if they're working or not. But don't let go of the reality of your ultimate dream.

You can use your vision to explore together as you support your team in aligning your shared values.

Start with the Why

With all the finger-pointing going on, I knew that the culture of this practice was clearly rooted in scarcity.

That told me that the first thing we needed to do together was to go back to our foundational principles of abundant vision and rediscover the team's Why.

We gathered the whole team together, and I shared a Simon Sinek video called "Start with Why". In this video, Sinek says, "Imagine a world in which the vast majority of us wake up inspired, feel safe at work, and return home fulfilled at the end of the day." This was a deliberate and powerful way to turn everyone's direction from scarcity—blaming—to abundance.

Once the video had set the tone for an inspiring and fun learning environment, we began a discussion about the team's Why.

We discussed what each team member loved about dentistry. This abundant focus on gratitude energized the group and reminded everyone why they'd chosen to be part of this practice's family to begin with.

Then we talked about what brought patients to the practice for treatment and the importance of connecting with patients and diligently working together to address their needs. I am a firm believer in making patient-centered care a central shared value in practices—you can't go wrong with this one.

As we talked, we went through each of the compass directions together—moral, intuitive, historical, directional, and strategic—in order to create a unified "We are here" statement.

We used vision boards for this and had some fun. It amazes me sometimes to see what teams come up with for the practice, and it's wonderful to see teams pleasantly surprise the doctor.

And once we discovered that "We are here" together, we were able to take the next powerful step: I guided the dentist in mentoring his team through creating some new systems and team agreements.

Everyone recommitted to the new systems and centered everything in a patient-first mentality. It was exciting to see each team member bring accountability to this beautiful new company culture!

Yes, there was doubt and frustration and stress; these are a normal part of any major change. The bigger and more powerful the change, the bigger the stress.

I try to remind dentists and doctors to take care of their teams through this process and make sure they have plenty of emotional and physical support. People need to be heard, and they need both fun breaks and rest breaks. (Don't forget some drinks and snacks!)

But the dentist and his team began to see some shifts in culture right away, and that energized everyone in committing to the process. It was so exciting when everyone realized that they were learning and supporting each other together.

The vision of a team must look beyond current circumstances and any obvious shortcomings of current teammates to see the potential of the team. If you can confidently measure the vision of your team according to the above compasses, and you find them all pointing in the right direction, then you'll know that the vision is worth stretching for.

–JOHN C. MAXWELL

Lift as a Team

In my years helping practices like yours, I have met doctors who are at all different places in their careers.

Some are excited and love what they're doing but aren't profitable.

Others are profitable but are miserable with their team.

And some are living the dream: enjoying what they do while also making a profit.

Vision is unique, and so each of these successful practices are living a unique dream. But they all have something in common: each practice is a professional home, combining the best of both the professional and personal worlds in a visionary way.

In these successful practices, the professional who owns the business has taken on the hard hat of real leadership to build work families they can rely on—and they can rely on their teams, because their teams can rely on them. That combined commitment carries their practice to synergistic new heights.

Every practice is like a family. Every family has its own short-term and long-term triumphs and challenges. The best ones aren't perfect; they're just the ones who meet their challenges head-on and are ready to get a different result.

You and your team have an exciting new opportunity to learn how to build a way of being, a hard-working practice of mutual support that makes it possible for everyone to achieve more—and more joyfully—than you could separately.

Remember, when challenges come up—and they will; that's how you know you're growing!—step back a ring in the circle.

Re-center on your own personal Why, so you can help your team discover their shared Why and refine their cultural How.

A renewed vision leads to the deliberate creation of a blueprint for a new culture. Your vision will help you rebuild your systems, ensuring that you allocate your resources in a way that fits with your true priorities and dreams and that both nurtures and requires your team.

Then, together, you'll all be able to better use the tools to build a practice your work family will be happy to come home to.

Building your work family takes work and effort, but it's one of the best investments you can make.

Teamwork makes the dream work. If you can achieve your vision by flying solo, then chances are you're not doing anything worthwhile. A big dream requires a talented team in order to root in reality.

–JOHN C. MAXWELL

Chapter 5

Your Hammer and Nails

Communication Tools for Building

Now that you are building your team of builders, you need to give them the right tools for the job you want them to do.

The best blueprints are worth nothing if nobody can understand how to build them. When you need a doorway built between what your practice is now and your future success, communication will be your lumber, hammer, and nails.

Communication connects your visionary Be, your team's cultural Do, and that wonderful Have that we're working towards together. The steps between having builders ready to build and a finished practice home with smoothly functioning systems, financial solvency, and patient-centered professional care are built with these tools.

The connection that communication creates is what helps you create your finished home and keep it as beautiful as when you imagined it and planned out every room and window.

Leadership, business ownership, and communication are important skills which are not always taught in medical and dental schools, but you cannot successfully run a practice without solid communication skills.

Circle of Accountability

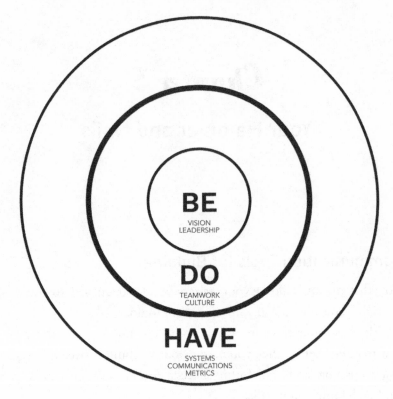

Trying to ignore the principles of true, authentic human connection is like trying to drive a nail with the palm of your hand—you can do it, but it's going to be far more painful and less effective than it has to be.

Law of Communication: Interaction fuels action. Effective teams have teammates who are constantly talking, and listening to each other. From leader to teammates, teammates to leader, and among

teammates, there should be consistency, clarity, and courtesy. People should be able to disagree openly but with respect. Between the team and the public, responsiveness and openness is key.

–JOHN C. MAXWELL

I've worked with many growing leaders like you who push through initial discomfort to open up their compass circle to authentic connection with their team and are blown away by how powerful this single principle is in practice. Communication is a tool that really works! Furthermore, it's a valuable skill that will bless your life and the lives of your team members outside your office.

As you identify with people and relate to them, your influence naturally increases. As you relate to each individual and with your team as a group, they will be more receptive to connecting with your vision, culture, and priorities, and they will show up for you.

We're going to talk about how people sometimes use their tools to tear down and how to use them to build up instead.

Let's build you some tools and show you how to use them!

Nailing It: Using Active Listening to Build Connection

Active listening gives you a big advantage as a leader and a professional. It means that when your team or patients have a conversation with you, they'll feel heard—like they've connected with someone who understands their wants and needs. This creates the opportunity to help others and increases our influence a great deal.

We do not communicate just to exchange information; we communicate to demonstrate the worth of others. Conversations are had on the spoken and unspoken level, and only active listening engages both conversations at the same time. Here is how to practice it.

First, seek to understand the person. Focus on not only what a person is telling you, but also the possible reasons why they are telling you. Be mindful that much of what they are trying to say is unsaid.

Second, ask specific questions. This does not mean asking "What does that mean?" after everything they say. If someone is having a hard time finding the right words, that question may not bring clarity.

Instead, you can try to help them articulate their thoughts and feelings by asking specific questions about what they are saying. For instance, if a team member says that they are not sure about a new process in your practice, you can ask "What about it bothers you most?"

These specific questions go far to demonstrate that you are attending to their words and that you care about their answers.

Connection is why we're here; it is what gives purpose and meaning to our lives.

—BRENÉ BROWN

Third, restate what has been stated. Make sure everyone is on the same page. Practice saying, "Let me see if I understand," and then restate what they have said, in your own words. If you did not understand, be open to their correction.

This kind of active listening exchange is a fantastic thing to practice, because whether they agree or disagree with you, they will feel like you have worked to hear them.

Good Doctor, Good Team—But Terrible Communication

Dr. Garcia brought me in to help him with his practice after the breaking point: a patient handoff had gone awry, and the patient had sadly communicated to Dr. Garcia that she had been so uncomfortable with the conflict she'd witnessed at his practice, that after years of being his patient, she was going elsewhere. Dr. Garcia had known things weren't great between his team members, but losing one of his longtime patients was a wake-up call that spurred him into action.

"They're good team members," Dr. Garcia told me. "I thought I was careful when I hired them, and they're each qualified to do what they were hired to do. But things still aren't working."

With that in mind, I started observing the practice, to see if there were patterns that would reveal what the core issues were, so I'd know how to help the dentist fix it.

What I found was that Dr. Garcia was right, about both the quality of his team members and the state of the practice. This particular combination usually indicates a common problem: a breakdown in communication.

Communication skills are foundational to a good practice, and yet their use can elude many otherwise excellent professionals, and their absence will bring down a good practice.

The thing to remember is that doctors and dentists aren't taught team communication skills in school. The communication that medical and dental schools teach focuses on communication between the professional and the patient. But team members aren't fixing each other's teeth—they're trying to work together, all day long, to run a practice and take care of people.

That's a different set of communication skills that they don't teach you in school, and when a practice is missing good communication, that absence will become uncomfortably obvious to everyone who comes into contact with that practice: the professional, the team, and the patients—especially the patients. If you think your patients don't notice the tension in your office, think again.

The patterns I observed in Dr. Garcia's office were like a chart of the progressive problems resulting from lack of communication, and, like many issues in practices, it started at the top, with the leader.

Dr. Garcia would try to tell his team what he needed or let them know about mistakes they'd made, but because he didn't know how to do it effectively, he didn't get the results he wanted.

Like many other professionals, he thought that the problem was that he needed to work harder to get his team's attention and help them understand how serious he was. His solution? To double his intensity and raise his voice.

And that's what happened, time after time. When there was a problem at the practice—a mistake made with paperwork or handoff, a personnel issue, a hiccup in training—Dr. Garcia felt so frustrated and overworked that he would yell louder about the problems he was feeling personally attacked by, and then he'd just walk away. He didn't offer his team alternatives or support.

I call this approach *yell and tell*. It's a natural response for frustrated humans, and it's also a terrible way to run a practice. Nobody does well being shouted at, especially not kind and competent people.

That's what had happened here at Dr. Garcia's office. They had reached the stage of the yell-and-tell cycle that I call the *cold shoulder phase*. Everyone had shut down and wasn't speaking to each other anymore, because they were trying to prevent more conflict in an already high-conflict office, where mistakes would lead to Dr. Garcia verbally beating them up. That growing company culture of feeling like they couldn't do anything right and work was a scary place meant that communication-dependent processes like patient handoffs were suffering.

Yell and tell typically leads to a feedback loop of failed communication, because the more people are yelled at, the more they shut down. The more they shut down, the less they communicate with each other, and that lack of communication leads to more dropped balls and costly mistakes, which upset the doctor or dentist, and so it spirals.

Again, Dr. Garcia was a terrific clinician, and the team members were all competent, kind people. But the communication and culture in their practice was so toxic that their skills were increasingly unusable.

Yell and Tell

A leader that resorts to yell and tell misuses their power, and instead of using influence to direct their teams, they simply come down hard on people. This is the difference between carefully placing and hammering in a nail or waving a hammer around and breaking holes in the drywall.

The "shout until I get my way" authoritarian style of management actually serves to undermine the kind of leadership that will inspire your team to be the best they can. Conversations are had on two levels; when a professional yells at their team, it tells their team that they do not matter and that they are not safe. When teams are belittled and scared, they withdraw and stop feeling safe enough to show up with the whole selves that a practice needs to succeed.

This behavior in a leader, when unchecked, will smash holes in the kind of culture successful practices share and will drive out the very team members you need most—the hardworking ones who have a natural gift for relating to patients.

Yell and tell, at its core, is a failure to communicate, and practicing good communication will prevent or diminish the circumstances that lead to this kind of behavior.

When leaders learn how to better connect and clarify and are willing to take the time to do so on a regular basis, they give themselves and their team members the opportunity to succeed where yell and tell fails.

The first step in treating this common issue is for the leader to be willing to change, so that they can create a bigger change in their practice's culture. This is why I begin with work on you and take you through remembering to base your interactions in gratitude and the recognition that your team members are a board of investors, without which your practice will fail.

The next step in treating these communication failures is to give the gift of connection. Your opportunity to drastically improve your practice is as near as your next conversation.

Starting at the Top

The good news is that these communication breakdowns are fixable! Here's how I got Dr. Garcia's practice started. The change started at the top.

This part isn't always easy for people—it can be challenging to show up and look in the mirror. Sometimes it's hard to acknowledge our part in broken processes. I helped Dr. Garcia begin by giving him John C. Maxwell's book *21 Laws of Leadership.*

We worked through the book by reading three or four chapters together, and then we'd discuss what we'd just read. When we started this process, Dr. Garcia shared the thought that it was his team's job to take care of him and that they were failing.

He said, "Now that I see what's happened, I can't take it anymore. There are too many problems. I'm going to fire them all."

I said, "That's fantastic!"

He nodded.

I added, "Except that you're still here. So what are you going to do about that?"

Dr. Garcia looked stunned.

Then—credit to him—he smiled and said, "I think you're right."

"You need to solve your communication issues," I told him, "because if you don't, then you will keep having the same issues you're having now, no matter how many people you hire and fire."

I've had this same conversation with team members at other practices too, when they've complained to me about their company and threatened to quit instead of working on trying to make things better. I tell them, "That's great; but you're taking you with you when you leave, so what are you going to change to make your future a better experience?"

That's the dark side of communication problems. You can't outrun them. You can't quit them. They will follow you around until you're willing to fix them.

The *bright* side of fixing communication problems is that the solutions tend to be universally applicable. You can take the same principles and strategies we work on and use them to improve your life at each new job and outside of work. I love how useful communication work is! It's totally transferable and can improve your life with your spouse or parents or kids right away.

We worked through the book, and the more Dr. Garcia worked hard to apply the principles to his own life, the more his eyes were opened to his part in how things had been. I would ask Dr. Garcia questions like, "How do you think this law of leadership applies to you and what you're doing with team members?" I was trying to help him see what he could do differently, moving forward.

I'm a big fan of focusing on the positive, so, as he started really showing up and taking responsibility in the way a leader needs to, I decided that he and the team were ready for some exercises to rebuild trust and connect to a new future.

Rebuilding Team Communications

Rebuilding the trust between Dr. Garcia and the team members was going to be possible, but I wanted to proceed with care.

I've helped a lot of practices through this healing process on their way to become terrific teams running successful practices, but it definitely feels tense in the beginning. Sometimes you aren't always sure how things are going to proceed, especially when there's been as much conflict as there had been in this practice.

This team had been working together for only a couple of years, so we started with something fun, something not connected to dentistry, just to get everyone loosened up and connecting.

We started going around the room, and I started asking questions for each person to answer: What's your favorite food? What's something about you that maybe nobody else knows? What are your strengths? We started with talking about who we each were, and then gradually I moved them into talking about why they were here, working at a dental practice.

Then I had Dr. Garcia take the lead. He apologized for his lack of leadership in the past and committed to creating something better moving forward. This kind of ownership and amends is the core of real leadership, and I was really proud of him for taking that step with his team. It went far in re-opening those bonds of trust that had been closed for some time, and that made the next part possible.

Dr. Garcia shared his vision of what he wanted for his practice, and what his expectations were. Then he and the team worked together to define expectations for each team member, to create future success for every person in the practice.

We finished up this trust-building session with an exercise called *Start Stop Continue*.

In Start Stop Continue, each person wrote down one thing they wanted to start doing that the practice hadn't been doing; one thing that was a bad habit they wanted to stop; and one thing they did well and would continue doing.

As each team member read aloud their Start Stop Continue to the group, we would try to make sure to give grateful shout-outs to other team members.

That gratitude and public appreciation was a wonderful way to close the day on a positive note, so that team members could come back the next day and keep working forward.

Great Change Doesn't Happen Overnight

I've helped practices in crisis for decades, but I have to admit it still affects me when I walk into a practice that's this tense. I can feel the fear people have, because they don't know what's going to happen. Sometimes I share some of that fear: will my help be well-received?

Fortunately, I'd spent some time getting to know Dr. Garcia's team before we began working on these communication and team exercises. I had been able to make friends with each of them on some level, so that they knew that I knew their story and that I wanted the best for them.

Respect for each person is crucial. Part of what makes a yell-and-tell work environment stressful is the lack of accountability and the feeling of helplessness around conflict. I try to create a contrast with that by asking each team member's permission to continue working with them and by inviting them to be part of the process.

Often this will include me asking them, "Hey, do you guys want to get better? Or do you want to continue living and working like this? How long do you want to do this?" I'll know that I've connected with them when people start nodding and warming up to the idea of being willing to do the work required to rebuild a practice family's connections with each other.

And even when everyone is ready and willing to do the work and when we've done the trust exercises together, there are still wild card moments. When problems have existed in a practice for a long time, I find that sometimes we have to take a break so that team members can do what I call *clear the air*.

Honesty is essential throughout this process, so I try to acknowledge people's experiences throughout the process. Clearing the air usually begins with me saying, "We're talking about some hard stuff today, and maybe some of you have had some trust issues with team members in the past. We'd like to move forward; but if anyone is not ready to, then let's just take fifteen minutes, right now. If you need to clear the air about something with someone in the room, let's go do that right now. You can do this yourself; I'll help facilitate whatever we need to do. Everyone else can take a snack break and I can help you work this out. But now is the time, because after today, we're moving forward from the past. So, you can either handle it now, or let it go forever."

It's a relief when people get up and go figure things out with each other outside the room. None of those conflicts have been secret, and everyone feels the strain of that tension. It's a good feeling for the whole team to know that people are taking ownership, working out their issues, and moving forward from being part of that kind of problem at work in the future.

The most important part of this process is the follow-through. It's vital for doctors and teams to know that these trust-building and air-clearing exercises I do with practices are not a magic wand. One conversation and apology can't make everything better; they are the beginning of real change that will bring a practice peace and success, and that real change happens slowly, in increments, as everyone keeps showing up, to work on making it right and working together towards something better.

It's not always easy, but it's absolutely worth it.

The Gifts of Connection

The Gift of Attention

True connection is the heart of communication, and connection requires focus.

Do you want to share your vision with your team? Then share your vision with your team. Make eye contact in each interaction. Put down what you are doing, and focus on them.

When two people take turns talking, that's a conversation. When people focus on each other and seek to understand, that's connection.

Conversations are forgettable; connection is powerful. The way to create this connection is through active listening, a practicable skill that can profoundly alter the nature of communication in your practice.

Imagine building alongside someone holding a hammer. Would you feel confidence in someone who isn't careful about where they're placing their nails or who is trying to hammer with one hand while texting with the other? Hammers are heavy, blunt objects, and that kind of inattention can turn one from a tool into a weapon.

Active listening means caring enough about the task at hand—and the person—that you put down everything else and focus on using the hammer properly. Respect the power of the hammer.

Part of this gift is seeing the things that aren't spoken. Body language is an important part of communication, but you'll miss it if your eyes are on a screen instead of seeing the person you're connecting to. Watch the body language. What's unspoken is just as much a part of communication as what's spoken.

Mentor your team in practicing this kind of connection, and make it a key part of your culture. Show them that you'll put down whatever else you're doing—your phone, your clipboard—and make eye contact. Show them that they and their concerns are important enough to you that you will focus on it exclusively. Ask them to do this for each other. Praise them when they do.

As you and your team practice this, you'll instantly raise the quality of experience in your practice, and your patients will notice this, and it will reassure them that they can trust you with their care.

The Gift of Curiosity

One of my favorite tools for better communication is what I call the *gift of curiosity*, and the way to give this gift is by asking open-ended questions and listening carefully to the answers.

A good listener is good at asking questions.

We all have different experiences and perspectives. Thoughtful questions demonstrate that we are committed to listening and establishing common ground. Questions bring clarity, which enables us to move forward with courtesy.

The best way I have found to give the gift of curiosity is to ask open-ended questions. If we ask only yes or no questions, the interaction doesn't always help us understand each other like it could and can sometimes begin to feel less like an interaction and more like an interrogation.

I know it sounds simple, but active listening is a skill many people need to practice in order for it to begin to feel natural. Here are some ways you can enhance communication by giving the gift of curiosity.

Start positive. This is something I learned from one of my mentors, Vicki McManus. She taught me that it's best to begin with the positive. You can do this by asking people, "What are you celebrating right now?" or "What's working?"

Listen to their answer, and then you can ask, "Why is that working?" Then you can go a little deeper by asking something like, "What's the system in place that makes that work?"

The real fun is when, together, you can make the connection between what's working now and what's possible in the future.

Sometimes that "aha!" takes them a little bit of time to reach, so I stay quiet and listen hard as I sense they are nearing that crucial moment of creativity. I give them room to come up with the new ideas themselves.

It seems like most people have specific ideas already on what could be improved and what they could do to improve things, and responsive listening gives them permission to start thinking about what else is possible.

The positive focus of this line of questioning elevates the attitude, so that it engages the same constructive thinking that people use for problem-solving. That's definitely something you want to encourage! Keep asking questions and creating new questions from their answers; it can help you both practice problem-solving.

Listen to the complaints. I like starting with the positive because describing what's working engages people's constructive forces more than fruitless griping will. But sometimes people just need to get some things off their chest before they're ready to move into that positive problem-solving space.

Here's how you can do it. When they complain, listen and ask, "What else?"

When they complain about the next thing, ask that again: "What else?"

I've found that if I am willing to use patient, active listening to make space for their feelings, then once they feel heard, they'll move into the more positive ownership space where the really great changes happen.

Often, after I've heard out several gripes—always listening and asking "What else?"—the team member will come to a point of realization on their own, where they'll say something like, "Oh…I guess that's something I could quit doing. I could do something about that, couldn't I?" Isn't that great? Just by being heard, many people will move themselves into the space of being ready to focus on the positive and to commit to changes to make that happen.

Reflect by rephrasing. There's an exercise I like to take people through to ensure they're actively listening and giving the gift of curiosity. I have listeners practice restating the last answer as part of the next question. This helps the listener practice focusing on the conversation and the speaker's stated needs, and helps the speaker to feel heard and encouraged to keep opening up for connection.

This is how a restating-the-answer conversation might sound:

Q: What would be the ideal schedule?

A: I'd like to start my SRP patients at nine o'clock.

Q: I heard you say that you want to start your SRP patients at nine o'clock. Is that right?

A: Yes.

Q: Why do you want to want to start your SRP patients at nine o'clock?

A: I want to start them at nine o'clock because that's when I have the best focus for scaling and root planing—afternoons are better for less complex cases. I have better outcomes when I pace myself that way.

Q: You have more focus in the morning for SRPs, and you want regular check-ups in the afternoons. Did I hear that right?

Sometimes people feel self-conscious about starting every reflected question with "I heard you say…" or "So, if I'm to understand you…"

It's okay to feel self-conscious. Do it anyway. There are so many miscommunications that could be fixed in the moment with a little active listening; it's definitely worth your time to restate answers so that the people you speak to feel heard and so that you both have every opportunity to get on the same page. That can prevent a lot of costly miscommunications.

Restating the answer is a wonderful tool that's widely useful beyond training. Everyone can benefit from practicing restating the answer—those for whom communication skills don't come naturally, teams rebuilding and maintaining productive connection, and anyone who's really busy running a practice and who needs to ensure they're on the same page for details of processes.

You can listen well without agreeing with someone. Active listening doesn't always require sympathy. You don't have to agree with what people are saying—and you don't have to correct them. Active listening will help people to think about what they're saying, and the reflection that good, open-ended questions provide will give people a mirror to look into, where they can begin to see their own part in how things have been and, hopefully, what their better part could be moving forward.

A good leader encourages followers to tell him what he needs to know, not what he wants to hear.

–JOHN C. MAXWELL

The Gift of Recognition

When we recognize what is unique and good in the people around us, we give them a gift. We tell them that we see them, that we value them, and that they are wanted. When you communicate, use tools that let you give this gift to the people around you.

Recognize and respect the language of the people that you're talking to. Often people will say the same thing and mean very different things; your team comes to you with a wealth of different life experiences and perspectives.

You can ground your gift of attention in abundance by working to see what is best in people and interacting with gratitude and respect. Each of us is totally unique and lovable, and finding what is positive about our similarities *and* our differences adds a quality of connection that cannot be counterfeited. People communicate far better when they feel safe and respected.

When you recognize what an asset that can be, and recognize the good in your team, you can move forward, using active listening to create a common language. That shared language will bring with it a shared purpose.

Respect different personalities. Some people like to have their interactions quick and respond well in the moment. But some people may need more time, maybe because their emotions could be high or because they're detail-oriented and need to think things through carefully. Create a way to succeed by honoring this difference, and build a culture that supports people in showing up as their best selves. It is okay to walk away for a little bit of time and come back to resolve a disagreement later, as partners instead of adversaries.

Respect emotions. Professionalism isn't about ignoring or hiding feelings; it's about connecting and meeting emotional needs in a smart and careful way. Your feelings and each team member's feelings matter and should be honored. Recognizing each person on this level and creating a sense of belonging in your practice for them will invite them to show up with their whole and best selves and do their best for you.

When you recognize and respect each person and what they offer, you create a place for each person in your practice. That's the kind of practice people will want to come home to.

The Gift of Praise

I cannot emphasize this enough: people crave praise.

All people want to be seen for what they have to offer and where they succeed. What you focus on grows, so if you want to increase this kind of confident success, don't let a little victory go by without making sure to praise it to the team member personally. Try to praise them in team settings, too.

In my experience of working in the dental field and in helping dental and medical practices to grow, I have not yet found a practice where team members didn't want praise and recognition, both from each other and from leaders like you. You and your practice can benefit enormously from this one simple but profound shift!

When you give feedback, be specific in your praise. This specificity is the most encouraging way to reinforce what you want to see more of in your practice.

It is nice to say, "Tiffany, good job on the instruments." A compliment like this is a good place to start. Better this than nothing!

But there is a lot of power in clarity. Try including a specific compliment tying the action back to the vision for the practice. "Tiffany, thank you so much for cleaning and setting up the instruments. You did a fast and thorough job, and it helped me so much."

When you do this, not only are you showing how much attention you've paid to Tiffany's work, you've also taught the rest of your team how they can better show up for you.

When You Feel Like a Bag of Hammers

If you have ever built anything with wood, you know that hammers are great for both building things up and for tearing things down. Same hammer, very different results.

I do not think any of us go into professional work or a human interaction intending to tear someone down or frustrate our own goals. But sometimes we still end up doing destructive things anyway, which can make us feel as dumb as a bag of hammers.

You can judge how effective communication is by how well it creates connection. Similarly, poor communication drives disconnection—that is, it tears people apart.

We are here to learn how to fail forward. Whatever we've done in the past as we struggled to lead will be redeemed by how we can show up for our teams and patients now. Your practice does not need you to be perfect, but it does need you to be present.

When you show up as your authentic self and truly connect with your team, you will be able to step out of whatever lies in the past and towards a far better future. This change is as close as your next conversation.

In the next chapter, we'll talk about how you can use your communication tools to build that better future by repairing conflict.

I know I'm ready to give feedback when:
I'm willing to put the problem in front of us rather than between us (or sliding it toward you).
I'm ready to listen, ask questions, and accept that I may not fully understand the issue.
I want to acknowledge what you do well instead of picking apart your mistakes.
I recognize your strengths and how you can use them to address your challenges.
I can hold you accountable without shaming or blaming you.
I'm willing to own my part.
I can genuinely thank you for your efforts rather than criticize you for your failings.
I can talk about how resolving these challenges will lead to your growth and opportunity.
I can model the vulnerability and openness that I expect to see from you.

−BRENÉ BROWN

Chapter 6

Systems: Your Load-Bearing Support

Some Assembly Required

What would you say if I told you that there was a way to improve your practice's efficiency and profitability while reducing your stress?

I help many practices with a variety of issues, at all stages of growth. Most of the professionals I serve come to me because they are struggling with stress. They have a variety of problems and have become overwhelmed by the issues in running their practice day to day. Despite investing in themselves, their team, and the equipment, they are not reaching their full potential.

But even the practices with solid leaders, excellent teams, and good communication are limited by their lack of supportive systems.

Running a practice without solid systems is like building a beautiful house according to a blueprint—sinking ample investments of time, money, and personal growth into developing the blueprints and builders, taking advantage of the wonderful views, finding all the best flooring and furniture and high-end appliances—but neglecting to build in supportive beams and load-bearing walls.

A house like this can have the best blueprints and builders, but then when you try to enjoy time in this home, the walls will keep falling in on you.

The bigger and more productive the practice, the truer this is. A house without support beams cannot be built very large or very high. Structures without load-bearing walls are limited by the weight that their drywall can support and cannot manage a second floor.

The buildings that soar and inspire have been built through innovative support systems that hold the walls in place and create room for beauty and inspiration. These systems manage the weight of the walls and literally take a load off!

Systems help us to move forward, to go as far as we possibly can. They enable us to work faster, smarter, and more strategically. A good system eliminates waste, while it also anticipates and removes obstacles.

To get the most out of systems, you have to make them a lifestyle not a one-off deal. They must become ingrained in your routine. Systems only benefit you when you stick to them.

—JOHN C. MAXWELL

Systems: The Load-Bearing Walls of Your Practice Home

So, what are systems?

They are the detailed processes of how every aspect of your office should be run. There are systems for patient processing, bookkeeping, and treatment management. Scheduling, phone calls, and clinical procedure all benefit from the strong support that systems offer.

Systems are the concrete expression of a visionary culture and the solid support structure of your practice home.

I know that you want to have financial success and excellent patient-centered care, and you need a way to determine if your practice is succeeding. Systems provide the manner, the maintenance, and the metric for this success. They are how you have your Have.

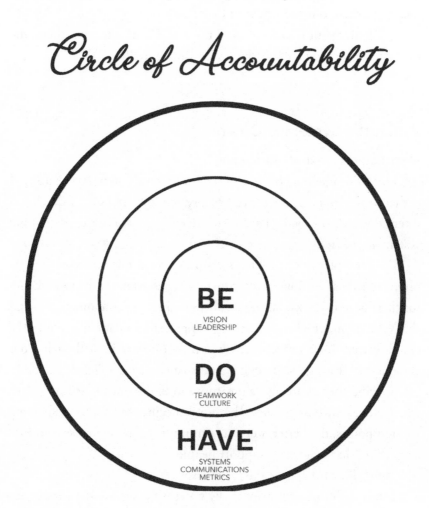

Circle of Accountability

In the circle of accountability, you can see that your visionary Be and your team's combined cultural Do must be expressed and measured through your practice's expanding Have. Your accountability flows outward from your vision, through your team and company culture, and takes shape in concrete, practical systems that prioritize the daily welfare of you, your team, and your patients.

The limit of what your practice can achieve is directly related to the quality of your load-bearing walls. A practice without systems will suffer; ones with them outperform the others.

The better your systems are and the better your team uses them, the more successful you will be. Systems raise the roof!

When the System Is Down

Dental offices are all about systems!

I have been helping practices for decades now, and what I've noticed is that nearly every dental office has a system of some sort. But, all too often, the system is being used ineffectively, not at all, or it's the wrong system altogether.

I've seen plenty of problems resulting from poor systems. People often try to make things work, substituting constant effort to make up for their systems' lacks, but it usually falls apart at some moment—and that's the moment when something happens like a patient being in the chair, waiting for a procedure, while their case is still at the lab. Poor systems will stress good practices, and that stress is a killer.

Specific stresses are also a great way to figure out the failure points in an office's current system. The more specific we can be in showing friction points, the better everyone can improve the shared system into something that will better support people.

Here's how I diagnose the problems:

I start with three colors of sticky notes. One is for what stresses out the doctor; the next is for what stresses out the team member; and the third is for what stresses out the patient.

Then I sit back and watch people move all around the office, filling out sticky notes and applying them to where that stress happens most.

Here are some examples of stress sticky notes that I might see in this exercise:

- a doctor's note on the patient chair: "the case wasn't here—we had to reschedule the patient and that bothers me"
- a patient's note on the same chair: "Being rescheduled is stressful"
- a team member's note stuck at the entrance to the sterilization room that says "there's always instruments here"
- a doctor's note on the table in the patient room: "I don't have clean instruments ready"
- a patient's note at the front desk: "I don't know how much to pay!"
- a team member's note in the back: "the 30-min appointments take 60 min and we're always running behind"
- a doctor's note on the front desk: "the schedule is too full one day and too empty the next"
- a team member's note at the front desk: "I don't feel comfortable asking for this payment from patients"

I love watching people put sticky notes all over the office. It's always interesting to see which places in the office stress out one group, and which places have stressors that affect all three groups.

In those areas where it's just one group that has a stress point, I find that group really enjoys getting the chance to open up about what system they're using right now in that area, how that's working for them, and how it relates to other systems.

Rebuilding better systems begins with thoroughly exploring what made the old ones break and why. I begin this process with some curiosity. I'll find a spot with a lot of the stress sticky notes and ask the people who left the notes to walk me through the system in that area.

For example, if I see a lot of sticky notes in the lab area, I'll ask the team to walk me through their current process for handling lab cases.

Often they'll say something like, "Well, we just check in the people as they come in and put them on the right side of the sink."

That gives me plenty of questions to ask:

"When do you check on that?"

"What do you do if it's not here?"

"What's your timeline for that?"

And, most importantly: "How's that work for you?"

Often, at this point, we can all see that this system isn't working very well—they've identified this area as a regular source of stress, and we've just explored some failure points of this current system.

Then we move into my favorite part: brainstorming solutions!

Law of the Niche: All players have a place where they add the most value. Essentially, when the right team is in the right place, everyone benefits. To be able to put people in their proper places and fully utilize their talents and maximize potential, you need to know your players and the team situation. Evaluate each person's skills, discipline, strengths, emotions, and potential.

–JOHN C. MAXWELL

We're Going to Need a Bigger Beam

Many practices I help either don't have systems in place, or their systems were installed at an earlier time and haven't kept pace with the practice's growth.

I'm here to help you make your practice grow, and as it does, it will outgrow whatever supports you have in place right now.

You've already invested so much in your practice and in your journey. These investments will slip through the cracks of your broken walls unless you shore them up with rugged, practical, well-maintained support.

The wonderful news is this: much of your day-to-day stress is due not to patient care issues, but to undersized systems that bottleneck your practice's potential success.

Poor systems are rife with uncertain expectations and muddled procedures. Nobody is sure what their responsibilities are or how to carry them out. This frustrates team members and stresses out professionals, because the lack of support results in the walls falling in—meaning you're managing crises instead of a business, and leaving you with no easy way to enact accountability.

Systems make things clear. They show everyone the most efficient and caring way to do things and unite leaders and teams. They make you more profitable and magnify your leadership capabilities. They help keep everyone accountable and create room for each part of your practice family to find their niche where they can add the most strength to supporting your practice.

If you want a second-story practice, you need second-story-worthy systems.

Once you invest in better support, you are able to open up the room for growth within your practice home. Your success will soar.

Effective leadership is putting first things first. Effective management is discipline, carrying it out.

–STEPHEN COVEY

Built to Soar

I've been helping practices establish and improve systems for a long time, so I have good ideas of what will work and what won't. It would be easy for me to just tell team members what kinds of systems would work for each part of the practice—but that would be my system, not their system.

In the long run, being given a system is nowhere near as effective as having people rebuild one together. That's the way to ensure your systems fit your practice's unique needs and strengths, and that everyone is invested in doing what it takes to make them work.

I guide this process through questions—first, questions to walk them through the current system together, and then once we've established the issues, more questions to help everyone brainstorm solutions.

Here's a sample conversation that I might have with a team as we all stand around a place where they've put a lot of sticky notes:

Me: "What if you had someone in charge of lab cases like this?"

Team Member #1: "Oh, we tried that once."

Me: "You tried that solution once? How long did you try that?"

Team Member #2: "We tried it for a few weeks."

Me: "What worked? What didn't work?"

Team Member #1: "We had a hard time getting that to work with check-in. We weren't able to make it work with our check-in schedule."

Team Member #2: "You know, we tried that when Sally was here."

Team Member #1: "Oh…and Sally was pretty disorganized. And she didn't like changing her check-in system."

Me: "Sally's not here anymore. Are you willing to give a system like this another try, to see if you might get better results?"

Team Member #1: "Oh! What if we checked lab cases two days before we needed them?"

Team Member #2: "I bet we could work that into the scheduling. I could help with that."

You can see that, at some point, my questions will help them start interacting with each other's ideas—and, even better, will lead to them volunteering to participate in the solution. That's the best part!

Nothing to Lose

Sometimes people resist change, even change for the better. That kind of resistance is a normal human kind of reaction, and it's why this exercise starts with a thorough review of what isn't working and why it bothers people.

What I'll remind people of, if this happens, is that what we have now has many stressors, and we're trying to salvage their work life from these repeated, predictable stressors. I'll ask, "Who's willing to try something different for thirty days to see if we can get some better results?"

It's important to try new things; it's also important to stick with those new systems for at least thirty days, to get a proper sense of their effectiveness. What you can learn in a month will guide you forward towards keeping, improving, or replacing that system, always helping you to hone what would work best.

Once people are reminded that they have options and that they will have support through the change, their brainstorming skills reactivate. I love watching people begin working together on ideas for that new system they can try for thirty days. Team members will start sharing ideas and volunteering who will be in charge of what. Sometimes, at that point, the process takes on a life of its own, and the biggest challenge is just making sure someone is getting all the good ideas written down!

It's wonderful to watch people step up. Once we've gone over what's not working as a team and established how awful that makes people feel, everyone is ready to start looking for a solution. I really love this part! The most important part of this moment is that people not only work together to name the problems, they also work together to create the solutions.

There's a System for That

Your practice already had systems in place—could it benefit from even better ones? The best systems are created by each team for their own use, and the more heavy-duty systems need to be customized to your team's unique combination of challenges and strengths—so I'll just include a few notes here on more generally applicable systems. These are very practical ways to build and maintain a practice home and staff it with a happy family.

Morning Meeting

Have a morning meeting and make it productive. Respect everyone's time by beginning on time, ending on time, and keeping it between ten to fourteen minutes. You may want to have a time keeper to ensure accountability for this, so everyone stays focused.

Don't just read the schedule. The meeting is to help team members organize collaboration on tasks they can't do alone.

Do review the previous day's production and collection goals and mention what worked, so everyone can apply better strategies moving forward.

The manager can share about which patients the office needs more information or paperwork on, who has outstanding balances, and who has any special concerns. This is a good time to review who has a signed financial arrangement or the next new patient opening.

This is also a good time for assistants to review who's on their schedule and who has outstanding balances and to make sure they and their family members are scheduled for their appointments.

Team members can check on lab cases and supplies, hopefully three days in advance.

These morning meetings are a great time to celebrate accomplishments, whether that's a payment being complete or someone doing a great job with a hard case.

Finally, the morning meeting is a great way to start off everyone's day on a positive, supportive note. Find and read aloud a good review of the office, share a positive quote, or praise your team. The options for positivity are limitless—just make sure they happen, because that kind of positivity is powerful.

Answering Phones

I spend months training the practices I work with on phone calls. Essentially, a ringing phone is a very good thing, and regardless of the question, the goal is to answer and handle the call well. Don't use a script (patients can hear that) but *do* answer with a great greeting and your name, and always get the caller's name first, no matter what they're asking about. The goal is to take control of the conversation in order to ensure better conversion and to maintain patients on our schedule.

Patient Processing

When bringing a patient from the back to the admin team, remember to use the patient's name. I like to think we all remember each patient and their name, but the reality is we sometimes forget either the first or last name. We don't want to make the patient feel we don't know them.

So, use their name and the admin person can pick that up on her check-out screen. Always review what was done today and what is next for them, even if what's next is the hygiene appointment.

This is a great communication tactic that teams love for front-to-back office or back-to-front patient transfers, once they get into the habit of doing it.

Scheduling

Scheduling is your office blueprint for how you want the day to go. It may not always happen, but you have a much better chance of that happening if you plan for success in reaching your goals.

I learned a long time ago from Dr. Bruce Baird about scheduling for productivity, and I believe in it 100 percent and have seen it work repeatedly.

A key concept is that there is no "magic". We have to discover a template that works for you, your team, and your practice goals. When a template that works for you is in place—it may take some trial and error—and you're off the rollercoaster schedule, that's when the magic happens.

Hiring

My motto is "Hire slow, fire fast." Be careful about who you hire and how. Often people interview differently than they work; one solution to this problem is to have your department interview the potential team member, to see if they can work well together.

Look for team players. Systems can be taught, but temperament can't. You need happy, can-do people.

Clinical Procedures

Make sure you make time to train, practice, and train some more. The team needs to learn the new things you do and speak about to patients. The more they understand, the better they can help you by helping the patients to say "yes".

Billing and Payment Plans

Each patient needs a clear understanding of their financial responsibility for each appointment, and the arrangements that they'll need to make.

This is a different conversation than one your team will have about treatment, and training your team in this takes time and practice. It's worth it.

Goal Management

I work with doctors and team to set and manage their goals. We do that by measuring those systems as well. If we are meeting goals, the system is working. If we are not meeting goals, it gives us an opportunity to look into that system and make adjustments and have success.

Team Member Training

It can be challenging to bring new people on board. Ensure that you're giving them every chance to succeed. Choose new hires carefully, and then invest deeply. Focus on one or two new things to train in per month, and praise them for their success. My mentor John C. Maxwell has a ratio for helping to train team members: 70 percent strengths (develop to the fullest potential), 25 percent new things (growth = change), and 5 percent areas of weakness (minimize weaknesses as much as possible, delegate).

Check Your Walls to Raise Your Roof

Systems are an amazing way to magnify your leadership and to make it easier for you to apply accountability to your practice's daily work with care.

But even the best systems are nothing without accountability. These are meant to support your leadership, not replace it. The best system is undone without a leader exercising accountability.

Human nature asserts itself through taking the path of least resistance; with careful investments in systems, you can elevate that path so that your team can serenely navigate through each day at an elevated level of efficiency.

Without training and re-training your team, your systems will eventually dwindle in neglect and leave your practice once again vulnerable to the vicissitudes of daily stresses and long-term wear.

You, your team, and your patients deserve better support and care. Building systems builds morale! Invest in systems to build room for amazing growth.

Chapter 7

Using the Tools You've Got

Conflict Resolution is How You Can Have Nice Things

We've already spoken about the principles of resilience, humility, and accountability. You have already laid the groundwork for creating a united team, good communication, and supportive systems.

These tools and principles are all about creating a practice that will be a wonderful home for people who take care of people, because people are the most important part of your practice.

They are your team of builders, your greatest resource, and your wisest investment. Your dream of a practice you can come home to cannot be realized without the work family who will run and fill it.

Good leadership and excellent business management are inseparable from taking care of your people, and treating them well will create incredible success for your organization.

People can be wonderful, but they certainly aren't perfect, and when—not if—mistakes and miscommunication bring conflict to your practice home, it's a leader's responsibility to correct the course.

Sometimes committed professionals like you interpret taking care of people as avoiding conflict, even in instances where a team member may clearly require correction or redirection. We want to be nice, but this can actually mean permitting a lack of accountability. Correction equals confrontation, and many people resist that as much as possible. We don't like this kind of interaction, so we avoid bringing up problems, hoping things will correct themselves.

When we do this, we are no longer doing our best as leaders and professionals in caring for the valuable people in our practices.

Why does this happen?

Fear of conflict.

This fear can keep diligent professionals like you from successfully bringing together all these principles together into a well-run practice.

Fear and avoidance can blind and deafen us, leading us to deny that the inevitable conflict even exists, because we do not want to see a problem we do not know how to solve. Denial allows conflict to grow and multiply into practice-corroding levels and will drive out the very people you most need to make your practice succeed. As the Cherokee proverb goes, "Pay attention to the whispers, so you won't have to hear the screams."

Conflict resolution is not something you'll learn in medical or dental school, but it is absolutely something that you need to make your professional home a happy place. The difference between dream practices and nightmare practices is not whether conflict happens; it lies in whether or not those repeated conflicts get resolved and how you resolve them.

This chapter will focus on conflict: how to spot it, what to do about it, and how to get ourselves to do what we know needs to be done.

Do Something about Mary

"Mary never has to make recall calls!"

I was assessing Dr. Jameson's practice to see where to start helping them turn things around. Part of my assessment includes talking to the professional, and part of it involves speaking to team members—after all, they're resident experts on what day-in, day-out life in the practice is like.

A lot of the complaints the team members made to me were similar to those that I've heard at many practices: Kendrah always wears the wrong color uniforms; Cindy always parks in the wrong spot; Bev never comes to huddle on time. These are standard small human-scale conflicts that I often help a dentist tackle by modeling how to gently but firmly correct a team member.

But as I continued speaking with the team members and heard the scarcity-fueled finger-pointing and avoidance, these combined reports began to paint a picture of a practice with considerable issues: fragile systems that kept breaking down, little accountability from the top down, and terrible morale as a result.

There was conflict everywhere, and nobody was resolving it. Small problems had been permitted to grow into huge, practice-altering issues.

The team members also shared with me that Dr. Jameson's assistant didn't have to play by the rules, and the rest of the team knew it.

Company culture is set by the owner-professional, and team members definitely notice when their boss isn't treating team members fairly or when team members aren't treating each other fairly.

If we want people to fully show up, to bring their whole selves including their unarmored, whole hearts—so that we can innovate, solve problems, and serve people—we have to be vigilant about creating a culture in which people feel safe, seen, heard, and respected.

—BRENÉ BROWN

These team members rightly resented what they saw as favoritism from the dentist to the one team member, because they were the ones who had to pick up the slack—for Mary, who wasn't doing her job, and for the dentist, who wasn't doing his.

This practice needed a lot of work, and I knew where to start: at the top.

I discovered that Dr. Jameson had a chaotic personal life, and that was leaking into his professional life. That was his responsibility to manage, but I also believed that it would be helpful to everyone if I could help him find success in resolving specific, practical conflicts in his practice.

We dove into the favoritism problem head-on.

I took Dr. Jameson aside privately and asked him directly, "Is Mary a favorite of yours?"

"No," he said, but he hesitated.

I asked him, "Do you know what your team's saying?" I told him the reports that I had gotten from multiple team members, of how other people had had to pick up her slack.

He admitted that he didn't have the same expectations of Mary that he did of his other employees and hadn't required the same accountability that he'd required of the rest of his team.

"Did you see how unhappy this makes everyone else in the office?" I asked him.

He sighed.

I said, gently, "If you knew this was a problem, why did you try to ignore it?"

Then he admitted, "I'd hoped that ignoring it would make it go away."

"Unfortunately, it has only made it worse," I said, and I could see what looked like a familiar expression of defeat come over his face.

Don't Circle the Drain

I could help this doctor fix his office's systems or advise him in how to bring hires onboard all I wanted, but the best practical fixes in the world wouldn't work without a leader willing to take accountability for enacting them. It would be like bringing in new furniture to a house built on a cracked foundation. We needed to start from the ground up.

Let's review our circle of accountability. We've done the Be (inspiration, vision) and the Do (culture and team) and we've talked about the Have (systems, communication).

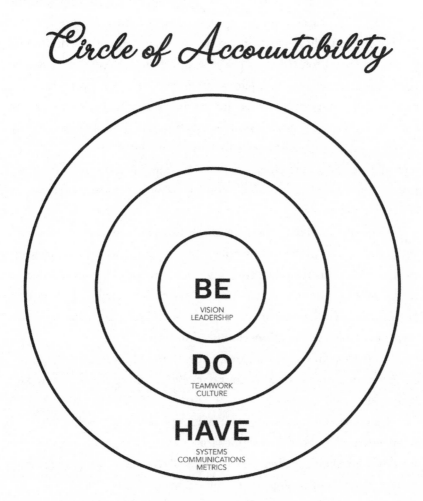

Circle of Accountability

BE
VISION
LEADERSHIP

DO
TEAMWORK
CULTURE

HAVE
SYSTEMS
COMMUNICATIONS
METRICS

In the story above, the problems that led the doctor to re-examination was a breakdown in systems and metrics. Further investigation showed problems in the middle tier—team morale—and also in the inner circle, which is where the professional's accountability begins.

The construction work that you need to turn your practice into a home and your team into a happy family begins with you and moves outward. You're the one responsible for opening things up and creating larger circles.

Whenever there is a problem in one ring, take a step back to the next ring in, and see if you can apply solutions there.

Ideally, you will always begin in the center, examining the dissonance between your vision for your practice and your current reality, so that you can embrace your own part in it, and move out from there, using improved communication to reconnect with your team and re-center your culture, and then key in your systems to rebuild for more specific support.

This beginning-with-self is a hard step, and a lot of people are tempted to skip it, which is usually how people end up in failing practices in the first place. After all, you can't confront others until you've confronted yourself.

Remember scarcity and abundance? Scarcity and shame will shrink your circle and restrict your practice's impact on the world. Shame keeps us stuck, keeps us from learning, and makes us want to blind ourselves to the problems going on around us. Shame is a terrible drain on the energy you need for creating powerful change and bravely taking on the uncomfortable conversations you need to have.

Don't let your circle pour down this shame drain!

Open it instead towards abundance and taking charge of making things better.

Resilience and abundance are what will make it possible for us to wholeheartedly take responsibility for change. Being willing to fail forward will give you the discernment and will to redirect your energy from things that drain to things that support.

This is why I start my clients off with learning from mistakes and walking away from shame and towards accountability, and then give them inspiration to work towards. I believe that the best way to help people open up to learning is to learn what a good leadership looks like, so that you can practice it yourself and, by so doing, inspire better leadership in your team.

You don't have to be perfect—only present!

Just acknowledging that you are trying to show up for your team will set you apart as a leader who's willing to do what it takes. Following through on real changes will prove it.

Recognizing Favoritism

Whether a doctor believes they're playing favorites or not, if a team perceives favoritism, then it's a conflict that needs to be resolved.

If you're getting feedback that this is what your team is seeing, then whether you agree with that assessment or not, it needs to be addressed.

Here are the two most common types of favoritism I see in practices I help.

Faint Praise

The first kind of favoritism is where a clinician truly prefers one employee over other team members.

Practices are made up of people. Owning a business is hard work. We are all human. It is natural to have some bias, especially towards a team member who is especially helpful or whose personality meshes well with yours.

If a team member is your favorite because they're doing all the right things, that's great! I'm a fervent believer that team members exhibiting great attitude and skills be encouraged and recognized.

Teams love praise, and I find nearly every clinician I work with could benefit from giving a lot more encouragement to their teams.

It's great to have an example of what you're looking for in team members, supported by your very clearly stated expectations for others, with rewards available to all team members who strive to improve, with the goal of building a high-performing team that holds themselves and each other accountable.

If this is the kind of favoritism that you may be exhibiting, then the core issue is that your team is feeling like your approval is scarce. They're operating from a feeling of not having the support they'd like. Favoritism is as unpopular among employees as it is among family members, and it's also as hard to hide.

To meet this conflict head-on, you need to move your practice from scarcity to abundance through how you treat your team. This is one of those few problems where the solution is to increase the initial behavior, instead of decreasing it!

Here's how to do it: Take that support and understanding you're offering to one team member, and open it up to include more people. Find something to appreciate and praise in every team member and reward them for it.

At the next team huddle, recognize them and thank them for their contributions. Amplify the kind of appreciation and support that every person wants; it will go a long way towards making your team feel like a family.

Running from The Ticking Bomb

The second kind of favoritism is created of compounded conflict avoidance.

The "favorite" team member fails to manage themselves or to perform adequately, or creates conflict of their own with other team members—but the clinician is so afraid of conflict that they don't hold this team member accountable for their work or their behavior.

Failing to address this kind of unacceptable behavior, or even rewarding it, is no way for your team to live. It's no way for you to live, either!

Sadly, conflict avoidance only creates more conflict and keeps you and your team living in discomfort or fear. Good team members, the kind you need most, won't be willing to tolerate that kind of work environment for long, and neither will you.

If you think problems are hard to handle when they're small, think of how much harder it will be to handle them when they've grown bigger.

When we don't handle the small stuff in a timely manner, it leads to a team breakdown in trust and communication, and that loss of trust damages our ability to create a practice that feels like home. The good team members quit; the bad ones will need to be fired; and patients will suffer in the meantime. The resulting turnover takes a toll on you, your practice, and the patients that you wanted to help.

But there is hope! You can turn this around.

I could tell Dr. Jameson was uncomfortable, and it would have been easy for me to back off here. Avoiding conflict is a very natural human thing to do, and even I am sometimes tempted.

But I'm not in the defeat business. The thing that keeps me going is knowing that facing this conflict would be a powerful step this doctor could take to make everyone's work life much better. I wanted to be sure to establish trust with him. None of us feel supported in change when we are feeling threatened or shamed; it is important to help shift from running away from a problem to running to a solution. It's important to get comfortable with discomfort, and using empathy and curiosity is a great way to do this.

The Law of the Chain: The strength of the team is impacted by its weakest link. When a weak link remains on the team, the stronger members identify the weak one, end up having to help him, come to resent him, become less effective, and ultimately question their leader's ability.

–JOHN C. MAXWELL

I said, "I have seen this before, and I am not here to punish you; I am here to help you. I am not going to shame you. We're just going to get curious here and observe some things about this situation."

He took a deep breath. "Okay," he said.

"How do you feel about this?" I asked.

"Really tense and embarrassed," he said. "I know that the team is unhappy with me."

"That sounds really hard," I said. "How does it feel when you come to work in the morning?"

"I dread more problems," Dr. Jameson said. "I worry about what people are going to do."

"Which person do you worry about?" I asked.

He shifted in his seat. "Well, all of them," he said.

"Mmm-hmm," I said, letting the silence invite him to keep talking.

"But…especially Mary. I know that the problems with Mary are causing trouble."

This was a great step, for him to admit this problem.

I said, "We need to talk about this problem very clearly and honestly so we can diagnose and treat it."

He took a deep breath. "Okay," he said.

"If you know Mary's behavior is a problem, and that it was making your team so unhappy, why didn't you hold her accountable?" I asked.

He got quiet.

Then he said, "It just has been going on so long that I wasn't sure how to fix it. So I tried to ask my team to ignore it so we could get by, and I tried to ignore it, too."

"Has that helped?"

He sighed.

"It's common for people to be ashamed of their fears," I said. "But I need you to list your fears. Get as specific as you can, so we know what treatments to apply, okay?"

This was language a doctor could understand, and—knowing that something better was on the other side of his discomfort—he was able to admit that Mary had ended up becoming a "favorite" because he was afraid of holding her accountable.

He told me that he was afraid of an emotional explosion from her and of how it might set off the rest of his team. He knew that people in the practice had been unhappy for some time, and he felt ashamed of looking unstable and unreliable.

Because he had been having personal difficulties in his life, he had not been as consistent in showing up as he should have been and was trying to curry favor with his employees by not holding them to standards that he wasn't able to live.

It was almost like accountability, in a way. But Mary had taken this laxity and run with it.

Ironically, it was because he had wanted a conflict-free, smoothly-running practice that he had tried to just let the small things go—but the multiple small instances of rule-breaking built up over time. Because he had already allowed Mary so much latitude, he did not know where to begin in fixing the problem.

Once Dr. Jameson saw the part he'd been playing in contributing to chaos in his practice, he reached deep within and got serious about wanting to make a change.

Pick Up Your Tools

Avoiding conflict is like owning a beautiful home and expensive tools, and then standing and watching rain come through the roof. Engaging in solving a conflict is like using your tools to fix something that's broken, something that's keeping your home from being what it could be.

If you're avoiding conflict, you're not picking up your tools.

Dealing with conflict is where leadership theory becomes action. Only by exercising these leadership skills can you create and maintain the culture, team, and systems that will permit you to blossom into your fullest professional potential.

Is there a good way to confront a team member? Yes. Note that I did not say it is easy or predictable. Dealing with humans and conflict hardly ever is. But there are principles and practices you can use to create the best possible conditions for conflict resolution at work.

Conflict Resolution: How to Do It

Clarification as the Key to Resolution

Resolving conflict begins with seeking clarification. You need to clarify to yourself if you are sensing a problem or not. You must be honest with yourself about the presence of conflict in your work life.

You can begin this by naming the confrontations you're afraid of facing. As you articulate your specific fears, you amass a punch list of tasks you can begin to tackle, whether it's planning to amplify your gratitude or your leadership.

Clarification plays another role, too. It helps us to approach conflict not as someone doing battle with an adversary but as a leader communicating better with a valued team member.

Thinking of the tough conversations we need to have as clarifications of our best practices and expectations and not as a tense dressing-down will help us to be willing to approach our team and will also ensure that our manner is as open, empathetic, and self-responsible as befits a leader who takes care of their people.

Communicating with a team member about work issues gives both of you a valuable opportunity to come to an agreement on how to best move forward, helping each other. Begin from a place of appreciating their innate worth, and assume the best. This can go far in helping to resolve conflict.

You will likely find that there was an expectation that you needed to clarify. If you make it clear what you need from the team member, they may change on the spot. "Oh, I never realized that's what you needed from me!" If, however, you find that the team member was aware of those expectations and of the team's needs and chose not to meet those expectations—that still clarifies things! You can use that information moving forward.

Rules of Engagement

So, now that you are starting from a place of valuing the person you need to communicate with and prioritizing how you will seek to give and receive clarification, here are some other guidelines for engaging with your team member in the most caring and professional way possible.

Focus on the issue. Get clear with yourself on what the primary issue is and stick to it. It may help for you to do some journaling to achieve this clarity.

If you are still struggling to name the core issue in a single sentence, then try role-playing with someone you trust. Get curious and observe.

If there are other issues, then you can have other discussions with this team member about those later.

You want to keep this brief and to the point. And, once the point is made, don't repeat yourself.

Focus on the now. Engage as soon as possible, and don't wait for a "better time". The best confrontation is brief and to the point and will not require that you set aside a large amount of time.

Sometimes people need a heads-up before a discussion, and you can choose to do that. But make sure to agree upon a time together, ideally within twenty-four hours of you identifying the need for clarification.

And once it is time to talk to your team member, be sure to put away every other distraction and focus exclusively on them.

Focus on the one. Confront people in private. A leader works to create opportunities for others to succeed, not fail. It can be hard for people to recommit to helping a team they have been humiliated in front of or to working with a leader who's humiliated them.

Focus on clarity. As Brené Brown says, "Clear is kind." Don't apologize for the confrontation; this is an opportunity for you and the team member to both do your jobs. Ideally, a practice family will strive to connect and clarify best principles and practices. Remember, this discussion is intended to be helpful for both of you. You do not have to apologize for it.

Also, please avoid sarcasm, whether spoken or written. We are striving for kindness and clarity, and sarcasm does not accomplish either.

Words like *always* or *never* are emotionally laden and are rarely accurate or helpful. Avoid them. Try to use *sometimes* or *often* instead, if you must.

Focus on solutions. Conflict resolution is not about an airing of grievances; it is about solving a problem. Focus on connecting with your team member. The best way to do this is to ask questions—"What happened? Why did you do that? How do you feel?"—and to offer suggestions.

Deal only with actions that can be changed. Give your team member a concrete suggestion for improvement, and try to phrase it in a positive way.

If you keep non-productive people, the productive ones become frustrated and leave. If you remove the people who don't add value, then the whole team gets better. It's just like trimming trees: If you don't cut the deadwood, eventually the whole tree falls. But if you remove the deadwood, the tree becomes healthier, the healthy branches produce more, and there's room for productive new branches on the tree.

–JOHN C. MAXWELL

For instance, instead of telling them to "stop fighting with the other hygienists," you can ask questions in order to work together with a goal of seeing the problem and hearing their ideas for a solution. If questions reveal what appear to be a communication issue, you could request, "Can you please ask other hygienists politely if they have already cleaned the room, and if they have not, please ask them to do so politely." Keep in mind that, depending on the team member, you may need to give a concrete definition of words like *politely* or even offer an appropriate script.

Focus on the positive. Highlight the person's positive contributions. Everyone has some kind of strength. Your goal as a leader is to invest in your people and direct them towards fulfilling their potential. Begin with what they are already good at, and go from there.

Feeling appreciated goes a long way towards bringing resolution, and it is a beautiful, abundant way to begin and end every clarification.

Firepower: Why Firing Employees is Essential to the Health of your Practice

I put this chapter where I did in the book because I want you to have had every opportunity to see where and how your own responsibility should have been applied in building opportunities for success for your team and your practice.

We have now covered leadership, teamwork, communication, systems, and conflict resolution. These are all the things to try first.

Everyone has a place where they fit best in a practice, where both they and the practice will thrive. Mentoring and maintaining a team requires a commitment to the flourishing of both your people and your practice. But as my mentor John C. Maxwell says, "A great dream with a bad team is nothing more than a nightmare".

You already know that keeping deeply problematic team members can damage what is best about your practice. Not only will continued conflict affect your peace of mind, it will also affect the best part of your practice: the people.

The very people you need most, who are most invested in hard work and organization and integrity, will be the first to sense when a practice is spiraling into conflict, and they will be the first to leave.

Nine times out of ten, seeking clarity will result in finding out that expectations were not clear, and the newly clarified expectations will bring solutions. But sometimes clarity brings us to the place of understanding that a team member is not working out.

Leadership here means owning that you may have made a mistake as a business owner—or that you did the best you could but ultimately the team member chose not to show up. Either way, it's on you to make it right.

Here is how.

Ready, Aim: How to Fire

This is the ultimate confrontation, one that many professionals dread. I'm going to give you nuts-and-bolts practical tips on how to perform this task. These are essentially the same rules of engagement as you would use for any confrontation, but with additional insight.

Clarity Brings Commitment

Many of your misgivings about this important task can be put to rest as you seek clarity and reassurance for why it's essential to fire employees who are not working out and why you need to fire this employee in particular.

Firing someone does not mean you hate them. It means you have recognized that their best good is not served by their participation in your practice.

Do not succumb to the temptation to begin strong and end with turning the attempted firing into a warning.

Leaders do not threaten to fire an employee in order to extract different behavior. If you believe a team member can change for the better, then follow the platinum rule and create an opportunity for success.

But if you are convinced that it is time to end this professional relationship, end it firmly and kindly.

Either way, the goal here is to solve a painful problem, not to create another one. Commit and follow through.

Teamwork makes the dream work, but a vision becomes a nightmare when the leader has a big dream and a bad team.

—JOHN C. MAXWELL

Practice Makes Perfect

Firing someone is a leadership procedure. Role-play your intended discussion with a willing volunteer to build your confidence, so that you can commit to the process.

This is an especially good strategy if you are afraid of drama. Practice saying, "This isn't working. I want the best for you, and it isn't here."

Hire Slow, Fire Fast

Once you know that someone needs to be fired, act on it quickly. Avoid the temptation to evade accountability through procrastination.

The most common mistake I see professionals commit here is to draw out the firing process.

Some are trying to be nice, putting off as long as possible actually having to say, "You're fired." It is far more painful to draw these conversations out. Kindness requires that you get to the point as quickly and straightforwardly as possible.

Others take the opportunity to make a speech. Remember, you are here to solve a problem. This is not the time, place, or person for airing grievances. Be professional and kind, and save those emotions for later processing.

Don't Participate in Drama

The biggest concern I hear from professionals learning to fire well is, "But what if they cry?"

Between you and me, it seems like male professionals worry the most about this. Emotional displays can be very disconcerting!

Take a deep breath and re-center yourself in the platinum rule: they deserve their best good. There is something out there that is a better fit for them, where they will succeed and be happier. Giving them the opportunity to remain a part of your team practice will not help them. It will simply keep them stuck in a place that's a bad fit. Let them go.

It is natural for people to cry when they are being fired. It is also common for some of the people who cry to attempt to use their emotional distress to change your mind.

If this happens, here is what you can do: hand them a box of Kleenex, and say—kindly and professionally—"Let me know when you're ready to continue."

And then wait. Resist the urge to meet their spoken or unspoken demands, and do not respond to begging. Wait for them to pull themselves together, and then continue.

Moving Forward into Something Brighter

When you fully commit to making your practice the kind of fun, happy practice that your team and patients are happy to come home to, then you won't be willing to tolerate the things that threaten that atmosphere. Honesty will bring you the insight and motivation to resolve the conflicts that stand between your current reality and your vision.

You can control only your part in these interactions; the rest is up to the other person. But when you begin with clarity and proceed with kindness, you will create a culture where people can grow from their mistakes and become something more. That is the kind of culture the best people want to be a part of.

I believe that all people want to succeed and be part of something great. If your focus is on appreciating people's contributions and offering direction and support, then your team will usually respond well.

Every practice is like a family. Like families, each practice has its own short-term and long-term triumphs and challenges. And, also like families, the best and happiest ones are not perfect; rather, they are those who are willing to try to meet their challenges head-on and are committed to do the work to create a better situation.

Chapter 8

Coming Home to Your Better Practice

Leading for the Long Haul—and Loving It

You did it! You showed up.

Some of these ideas are things you were already doing, and some might have been new. That's great. Keep reading and planning so you can build comfort with discomfort. Start with where you are, pick one new thing to try, and after you've done that, add in the next change. You're ready to make your practice home a well-built, happy home.

Here is a summary of the concepts we've gone over in this book. See where you are ready to dive in a little deeper, and then get to work!

Show Up, Take A Look in the Mirror, and Fail Forward

We all make mistakes; it's part of being human. Mistakes are some of the best business lessons we can learn! Mistakes will teach you who you are, what you're made of, that you can survive looking at your weaknesses, and that you can grow in your strengths. The best people in the world make mistakes. Maybe you should try making some too!

The real obstacle between you and doing better is not the mistakes you make; it's the perfectionism that makes you hesitate to try again.

When—not if—you and your team make honest mistakes, just try again. Every failure is a step closer to success. Plan A is overrated, and there are so many other letters in the alphabet.

The more you do this, the stronger you'll get, and the better you'll model resilience for your team. That will help create the kind of culture that welcomes real people, where people feel happy and safe working on being a little better every day.

The Law of the Big Picture: The goal is more important than the role. Members must be willing to subordinate their roles and personal agendas to support the team vision. By seeing the big picture, effectively communicating the vision to the team, providing the needed resources, and hiring the right players, leaders can create a more unified team.

–JOHN C. MAXWELL

Build a Blueprint for Every Day

Get a vision, and then put your vision to work! Set clear goals for what you want to accomplish every day. Many of the team members I talk to tell me they waste time at work because they aren't sure what work is a priority and what isn't.

As a leader, you get to work with your team to set clear goals with concrete follow-through. Make sure everyone knows the priority of each task and what each person's role is in accomplishing them. The more clearly you communicate this, the more help you can give and get.

The best part of a leadership blueprint comes when you can share vision and goal-setting with your team. Offer your team opportunities for self-development, and let them give increasingly expert input as a result.

Remember You Are Leading Leaders and Not Babysitting Employees

Accountability is important, but don't micromanage. People perform best when they have a leader who has their back, not a boss looking over their shoulder. Second-guessing your team members' decisions actually has the effect of reducing and not increasing their accountability and growing leadership abilities.

If the goals you make with your team are clear enough, and if you've hired carefully, then trust your team to navigate achieving what needs to be done. Respect their abilities, and respect their time—which leads me to my next piece of advice about leading leaders.

Don't waste your team's time with extraneous meetings. Notice that I said *extraneous*. It's important to have morning huddle every day; it's equally as important to keep it brief.

Every meeting needs to have the very clear goal of helping to communicate goals and offer support, and once meetings go too long or happen too often, they stop being helpful and start being disruptive.

Make sure you have an agenda for your meetings, and invite only those who must be there. Start on time, end on time, and stay on task.

Happy Families Work Together

Families who have fun together, work together.

Happiness is contagious! Enthusiastic, positive team members are worth their weight in gold and will help anchor your practice's culture in a good can-do attitude.

When you hire slowly and carefully, make sure your potential employee shows the kind of attitude that will contribute positively to making your practice home a happy one. Given the choice between an employee with high skills and iffy attitude, and a cheerful team player who is eager to learn, I go with the latter. Yes, it's that important.

Keep an eye and an ear on the happiness of your team. If something is wrong, be the kind of leader people feel comfortable sharing their concerns with, who can be relied on to help. Remember, if you listen to the whispers, you won't have to hear the screams.

One way to invest in your practice family's happiness is to provide them with a pleasant place to work. People feel better in clean and stimulating environments. Beauty around us invites us to answer with beauty from within.

This doesn't have to mean spending lots of money on interior decor; it does mean showing an effort and inviting your team's input on what could make your office a more pleasant place to spend the day. Your patients will thank you for it, too. It doesn't take a lot of money to demonstrate a sincere interest in improving their surroundings and comfort.

Another way to increase the happiness in your team is to show them that their input is appreciated. You can do this during your brief, goal-oriented meetings; you can recognize them publicly and privately for their contributions. Above all, invite their input by asking questions, listening to their concerns, and inviting their suggestions. Then, whenever possible, implement their suggestions.

This is a concrete way to show your team that your practice really is a group effort and that you truly value them. When you welcome this kind of 100 percent participation—including hearing out their concerns—you will get employees who show up 100 percent for you. What an amazing investment!

Invest in Your People

Offer your team opportunities for self-development.

Law of the Bench: Great teams have great depth. Any team that wants to excel must have good substitutes as well as starters. The key to making the most of the law of the bench is to continually improve the team.

–JOHN C. MAXWELL

Team members who learn new skills don't just increase their own value as employees; they enrich your practice. As you guide your practice through this exciting transformation, make a leadership goal for yourself that you can support your team in getting the training they need to advance, whether through workshops, certifications, or conferences.

Invite them to learn alongside you in gaining knowledge in the latest treatments and tools. This is a terrific way to invest in yourself, your employees, and your practice. As they learn more, they will have increasingly expert input to offer during meetings and will grow into being the leaders that are the hallmark of the most enjoyable, successful practices.

Also, make sure to pay people what they are worth. Research by Glassdoor states that 35 percent of employees are so dissatisfied with their salary that they reported being willing to look for a new job if they did not receive a pay raise in the next year.

When you are setting team member salaries, make sure that their pay is consistent with what other practices in your region offer. We have already spoken about the intangibles that you can offer as a leader—clearer communication, better work environment—but it is hard to motivate people out of not having enough money. Pay them what they're worth. Don't lose great people because you didn't pay them enough.

Practice Being a Happy Family at Work

I've told you a lot about what unhappy practices have in common—now I'll tell you what happy practices look like, so that you can get a good idea of how close you are to coming home to a better practice.

Values

Happy practices have worked hard as a team to create their core values, and they write them down and display them. Those core values are a key part of the onboarding process for new team members, and usually those core values will help guide how that practice will approach problem solving and help people to feel united.

The most important core value I see in the best practices is the mentality of patient first, team second, and self third. The practices that operate in integrity with this value are able to reach greater success, because their priorities are centered in what will bring everyone the most personal and professional success.

Trust

A happy practice is happy because people work on creating happiness.

Happiness doesn't just happen. The reality is that there will be upsets, disagreements, and tough conversations; no practice will ever be totally free of those. One of the most stressful things about conflict is the fear of not knowing how to make things better. The difference is that happy practices agree on durable processes for resolving upsets and tough conversations. A practice that has an established, agreed-upon process for resolving conflict is a practice where people can trust that things will be okay and where they know how to work together to resolve conflict well.

The best conflict resolution processes embody personal respect. What I see most commonly is a process where both parties are invited to try to work things out privately and have the option of asking the doctor or office manager for help with resolution. The best practices do not tolerate gossip—that's a fast way to destroy trust and seriously weaken a process. Issues need to be swiftly resolved, before they ever get to the point of people gossiping about them.

Fun

The teams I see that take patient care to the next level are those that play together.

Fun is a great way for teams to bond, and celebrating team accomplishments does a lot to help people remember that patient first, team second, self third ethos while also feeling personally appreciated.

Fun activities can be planned with respect to the individual preferences of team members. You don't have to require people to be best friends or to attend a Forced Fun Day. But it is nice for people to have opportunities to get to know each other in a relaxed way and to find things in common.

Happy practices encourage teams in enjoying things that people can opt into or plan themselves spontaneously: going out for Mexican food after work or an office beach day or a trip to an escape room.

The fun isn't about making everyone like the same thing or having to be good at the same skill—use the fun activities to celebrate the strengths each individual brings to the table!

When everyone knows they're welcome, safe, and supported in being the best professional and team member they can be, then you'll have created a happy practice that everyone can come home to.

The Law of Mount Everest: As the challenge escalates, the need for teamwork elevates. Focus on the team and the dream should take care of itself. The type of challenge determines the type of team you require: A new challenge requires a creative team. An ever-changing challenge requires a fast, flexible team. An Everest-sized challenge requires an experienced team. See who needs direction, support,

coaching, or more responsibility. Add members, change leaders to suit the challenge of the moment, and remove ineffective members.

–JOHN C. MAXWELL

You Can Do This

I know it hasn't been easy. Looking at ourselves and doing things differently can take a lot of energy. You have pushed through your fear of failure, and you have worked hard being willing to try new things.

You can keep trying out these ideas and practicing these principles. When you are ready, you can start to put these concepts and suggested changes together to improve your practice.

Remember, it is normal to feel overwhelmed and unsure sometimes, especially when trying new things.

But you can do this! You made it through school, and you have a heart to serve people with your specialty skills. You have a work to do that people need, and the more you can improve your practice, the happier you can be while doing it. And as you incorporate more of these principles into your practice, your work family will grow, and your professional happiness will deepen. I believe you deserve this, and I can't wait for the morning you wake up, excited to take on the day with a terrific team at your back.

You can create this, and when you do, you'll know that you're home. Enjoy!

Further Reading

Chapter Two: The Compass Circle of Accountability

Davis, Karen. "57 Dental Practice Management Tips: The Definitive Guide," #5. Delmain.co. https://delmain.co/blog/57-definitive-dental-practice-management-tips/ .

Compass: *https://simple.wikipedia.org/wiki/Compass_(drafting)*

Maxwell, John C. *The 17 Indisputable Laws of Teamwork: Embrace Them and Empower Your Team.* Bhopal, India: Manjul Publishing House, 2013.

Brown, Brené. *Dare to Lead: Brave Work, Tough Conversations, Whole Hearts.* New York: Random House, 2018.

Maxwell, John C. *The 21 Indispensable Qualities of a Leader.* Nashville, TN.: Thomas Nelson Publishers, 1999.

Covey, Stephen R. *The 7 Habits of Highly Effective People.* London: Simon & Schuster, 2005.

Maxwell, John C. *Leadership 101.* Nashville: Thomas Nelson, 2002.

Covey, Stephen R. *The 7 Habits of Highly Effective People.* London: Simon & Schuster, 2005.

Chapter Three: Build Your Builders

Maxwell, John C. *No Limits: Blow the Cap off Your Capacity.* New York: Center Street, 2018.

Maxwell, John C. *The 17 Indisputable Laws of Teamwork: Embrace Them and Empower Your Team.* Bhopal, India: Manjul Publishing House, 2013.

Brown, Brené. *Daring Greatly: How the Courage to Be Vulnerable Transforms the Way We Live, Love, Parent, and Lead.* London: Penguin Life, 2015.

Maxwell, John C. *The 17 Indisputable Laws of Teamwork: Embrace Them and Empower Your Team.* Bhopal, India: Manjul Publishing House, 2013.

Maxwell, John C. *The 17 Indisputable Laws of Teamwork: Embrace Them and Empower Your Team.* Bhopal, India: Manjul Publishing House, 2013.

Maxwell, John C. "Finding a Vision's 'True North'." Johnmaxwell. com. January 17, 2011. *https://www.johnmaxwell.com/blog/finding-a-visions-true-north/.*

Maxwell, John C. "Vision: From Start to Finish." Johnmaxwell.com. June 11, 2011. *https://www.johnmaxwell.com/blog/vision-from-start-to-finish/.*

Chapter Four: Hammer and Nails

Maxwell, John C. The 17 Indisputable Laws of Teamwork: Embrace Them and Empower Your Team. Bhopal, India: Manjul Publishing House, 2013.

Maxwell, John C. The 21 Indispensable Qualities of a Leader. Nashville, TN.: Thomas Nelson Publishers, 1999.

Brown, Brené. "Daring Greatly Engaged Feedback Checklist." Brenebrown.com. 2017. https://brenebrown.com/downloads/.

Chapter Five: Systems

Maxwell, John C. "The Value of a Good System." Johnmaxwell. com. June 11, 2011. https://www.johnmaxwell.com/blog/the-value-of-a-good-system/.

Maxwell, John C. *The 17 Indisputable Laws of Teamwork: Embrace Them and Empower Your Team.* Bhopal, India: Manjul Publishing House, 2013.

Covey, Stephen R. "Habit 3: Put First Things First." *Www.franklincovey. com. https://www.franklincovey.com/the-7-habits/habit-3.html.*

Chapter Six: Conflict Resolution

Brown, Brené. Dare to Lead: Brave Work, Tough Conversations, Whole Hearts. New York: Random House, 2018.

Maxwell, John C. The 17 Indisputable Laws of Teamwork: Embrace Them and Empower Your Team. Bhopal, India: Manjul Publishing House, 2013.

Brown, Brené. Dare to Lead: Brave Work, Tough Conversations, Whole Hearts. New York: Random House, 2018.

Maxwell, John C. The 17 Indisputable Laws of Teamwork: Embrace Them and Empower Your Team. Bhopal, India: Manjul Publishing House, 2013.

Maxwell, John C. Teamwork Makes the Dream Work. Petaling Jaya: Advantage Quest Publications, 2008.

Chapter Seven: Coming Home to a Better Practice

Maxwell, John C. The 17 Indisputable Laws of Teamwork: Embrace Them and Empower Your Team. Bhopal, India: Manjul Publishing House, 2013.

Maxwell, John C. The 17 Indisputable Laws of Teamwork: Embrace Them and Empower Your Team. Bhopal, India: Manjul Publishing House, 2013.

Maxwell, John C. The 17 Indisputable Laws of Teamwork: Embrace Them and Empower Your Team. Bhopal, India: Manjul Publishing House, 2013.

Dickson, George. "20 Surprising Employee Retention Statistics You Need to Know." Business 2 Community. Accessed December 22, 2017. https://www.business2community.com/human-resources/20-surprising-employee-retention-statistics-need-know-01976494.

Made in United States
Orlando, FL
19 August 2022

21265780R00082